IN GOOD FAITH

IN GOOD FAITH

STEWART LAMONT

THE SAINT ANDREW PRESS
· EDINBURGH ·

First published in 1989 by
THE SAINT ANDREW PRESS
121 George Street, Edinburgh

All material contained within this book has been adapted and reproduced from the weekly column 'In Good Faith' written by Stewart Lamont. The publisher is indebted to the *Glasgow Herald* for permission to use these articles.

ISBN 0–7152–0636–2

British Library Cataloguing in Publication Data
Lamont, Stewart, *1947–*
  In good faith.
  I. Title
  200

  ISBN 0–7152–0636–2

This book is set in 9/11pt TIMES
Typeset by SB Datagraphics, Wyncolls Road, Severalls Lane Industrial Estate, Colchester, Essex CO4 4HT
Printed in Great Britain by Bell and Bain Ltd., Glasgow

CONTENTS

CONTENTS

STEWART LAMONT has been writing the *In Good Faith* column for the *Glasgow Herald* for as long as I have been editor, that is to say since 1981. He was one of my first signings and one of my best. Every Saturday he has stimulated, amused and infuriated our readers with his reflections on manners, mores and the spiritual life. He ranges widely, through politics and international affairs, and can turn his hand to the parable with great aplomb.

In his column and elsewhere he has written with enormous insight and authority on ecclesiastical affairs. To his understanding of issues he adds a keen news sense that does not exclude the human element. For this he has sometimes been criticised, but he is surely right, for the life of the Church consists of the lives of people and is not simply a matter of abstract theological debate. It is because of his capacity to marry an understanding of ideas with an understanding of people that he is, I think, unique among journalists working in Scotland today.

Arnold Kemp
Editor, the *Glasgow Herald*

ON SATURDAY, there must be very few *Herald* readers who lay down their paper without having been interested, impressed, stirred or annoyed by the article appearing under the heading *In Good Faith*. For myself I'm whiles among the admirers and whiles among the aggravated, but even when I'm featuring violently in the latter group I never cease to marvel at the skill in finding vital themes, at the freshness of the presentation, at the cannie touches of humour, at the gentle way in which the prodding is done in the sensitive areas. And to have another one ready for next Saturday!

I am happy indeed to think that a number of those weekly gems are going to be preserved in a separate volume, and I am proud to have been asked to write this foreword. Nothing I could say here could add to the value of the articles or enhance their attractiveness: so read on and enjoy at a sitting what up till now we had to get in bits and pieces.

Andrew Herron
Former Moderator of the General Assembly
of the Church of Scotland

IT MIGHT SEEM STRANGE that a Catholic Archbishop should pen these few words in favour of an author who has so clearly maintained a love/hate relationship with our Church.

He meddles in the affairs of all churches, and seems quite prepared to take the consequences—one of which is this!

I do like the way he tackles injustices which don't always seem big enough to merit the headlines, and the trenchant manner in which he prompts a thorough examination of conscience.

There are times when the *In Good Faith* column gives rise to a mild indigestion over the cornflakes, particularly when the author's grasp of religious affairs seems to cement the idea that Church life is chiefly about power struggles. That indigestion, however, is a small price to be paid when one considers the efforts and the influence wielded by one Christian voice in a society in which Christian values need to be affirmed and promoted.

Thomas J Winning
Archbishop of Glasgow

August 1989

MIND

Think pieces...

When the churches are gone religion will be simply all in the mind

Religion 200 years after the *Glasgow Herald* was 200 years old . . .

TO be able to conduct an uninterrupted interview with Glasgow's largest TOM Controller, you have to be down in George Square bright and early. The pinky hue of the eastern sky had begun to spill over the giant three centuries old building at the east end of the Square when I called at 7 a.m. sharp to meet him. The vast numbers of Glasgow citizens who use its facilities daily have probably forgotten that 'Major TOM' was the subject of intense controversy when it was first mooted way back in 2128.

First sketches of the TOM were shown through the television networks and negative feedback from viewers in the West of Scotland jammed consumer response computers in Brussels. But more than 50 years ago the idea of a TOM, or Transcen-dental Operations Module, was fairly new. There was nobody who remembered the days of churches where people assembled for religious ceremonies, but they resented the idea of a TOM replacing the function of the antique building set aside for sacred ceremonies.

For over a century the medieval churches which remained had been museums in the care of the European Sector, but it had proved impossible to balance their antiquarian value against the considerable costs of allowing religious practice to take place within them.

Most Victorian churches had disappeared—upkeep could not be justified as they were quite unsuitable for individual meditation. Despite many ingenious methods of providing tran-

3

scendental excitement, the TOM only came into its own in the mid twenty-second century.

Mordecai Macdonald was young to be a TOM Controller. At 30 he had amassed enough knowledge of transcendental experience systems to make him a contender for the job of running what was regarded by many as one of Europe's best Transcendental Operations Modules.

He had a lean face and dark eyes that might have come from either his Gaelic or Jewish ancestry. His gingery short cropped hair decidedly came from the former. His long nose came from the latter and more specifically from a genetic type unit near the Dead Sea.

For Mordecai it was a symbolic birthplace, for he was a direct descendant from one of the millions of Jews who had been evacuated from the Middle East in 1990. The Second Diaspora was more traumatic for the Jews of the twentieth century than the one which scattered their forebears 2000 years previously. Then it had been Roman revenge against an uprising—but the seizure and detonation of an Israeli atomic bomb by terrorists had made a second holocaust of the land that once was known as Holy. Two million had died and the world had hung on a heartbeat, and the sky had blazed like a thermonuclear sun standing still.

The event was known as the Day of the Dark Host. As if to remind him of the past, Controller Macdonald had a large video print of that moment on one wall of his office, which was in the basement.

The soft light did not discriminate between day or night. It helped create a feeling of timelessness. "I'm not in favour of reading too much into history," he explained. "Look at how that affected the potential of so many citizens in this very city. Catholics and Protestants developed their beliefs because of what happened in their history, not because of what they wanted to believe. I pointed out that Christianity had always stressed the idea of faith history (having got it from the Jews) and that Jesus was believed to be the intervention of God in human history.

"That is true," he laughed, as if relishing the chance to discuss theology so early in his day. "But that was one of the factors that contributed to the eclipse of Christianity. Being shackled to one epoch meant it had to change and adapt but try to reconcile this with harsh realities. This meant that some Christians followed Jesus as a Guru, others as a moral guerrilla leader and still others worshipped him as a perfect person. There were so many versions of Jesus, but only one can be true if you allow history to pronounce the verdict.

"For my part I believe the African Jesus would have won if it had not been for the Dark Host. I believe it provided a turning point. Faced with the threat it posed we somehow managed to break free of the old categories. If you like astrology symbols like Carl Jung did, you would say that it was the end of the epoch of the Fish and the beginning of Aquarius.

"Of course it hasn't all stemmed from that seed," he continued, pouring a glass of fruit juice and offering me a bowl of seaplant mousse into which to dip my bran biscuit. "My ancestors in the Scottish islands used

4

to farm seaweed and if they'd had our technology they could have made a dish like you're eating now. But they were limited by their technology. We solved the global food problem by applying that technology to the two thirds of the globe that is covered by water. The root of that technology was the discovery of fusion power.

"You see, two centuries ago they had electricity—but in order to make it they had to burn non-renewable resources and endanger people with fission systems. Now we have clean power with unlimited sources it takes the heat off yet another area of national and cultural competition."

"That doesn't explain the spiritual revolution which resulted in the collapse of the world's religions," I queried. "Don't you think that had more to do with the World Council of nations assuming power and nationalising religion . . .?"

"If there's only one governing authority, you can't nationalise—only internationalise," he countered with a twinkle. "But you're forgetting that was the result of evolution, not revolution. With money and microchips— that's how it happened. When the multinational firms saw that they were international, the minds of the people followed them."

Mammon replacing God? He didn't seem to take offence at my lack of enthusiasm for the system which had made religion into something you did in your home or in private or at its most social—in the privacy of a cubicle in Major TOM. "I suppose that would have been regarded as subversive by some governments in the bad old days," he said. "But that's not quite the way it was.

"Personal choice for a Western person used to be important. Overall control for the good of all was important to the communist. Now the two are combined. Technology means that the former is open to us and is organised by the latter.

"In the psychic realm it means that we are free to follow any set of images and symbols which give us the right mental feedback—and the State encourages us. Even to the extent of providing a TOM. Here someone can be advised of the systems available. Were you for instance more comfortable with a Mother fixation, I might give you a Catholic programme or a Russian Orthodox icon system. If you're not so visual, I could programme you into an Islamic based course."

"But surely that means the reintroduction of imposed worship?" I quizzed the Controller.

"Oh no! It means that we are selling the consumer what he wants for his psyche. We fill thought space but don't forget there are a lot of creative people preparing the programmes just to ensure there will be an adequate choice. The possibilities are infinite. Our video banks have material from all the world's religions. All you do is key in your psyche data and if offers you a wide range of mind expanding sensations."

He rose to conduct me round the TOM complex. The cube building is the base, with consulting rooms in the basement and the sides of the cube are a honeycomb of booths soft furnished with couch, video screen, audio input—and the article as common in every house as the telephone once was, the communications terminal, enabling me to key-in my needs.

Above the cubes was an egg-shaped dome of several hundred feet. At its top a small light gave a spacious feeling as the early ages might have felt entering a mosque or domed basilica. Glasgow's Taj Mahal transported you beyond the eastern sky to infinity.

"The great revolutions in human history have not been military," explained the Controller, "but in communications. Papyrus enabled the ancients to spread their religion to a wider audience. The printing press enabled Luther to start a Reformation —think how long it would have taken him to preach his way round Germany. The microchip has extended his idea of justification by faith alone. Previously you had to be part of a quarrelsome, uneconomic unit of orthodoxy known as a church. Now you can key-in your confession, supplication and intercession, in total privacy."

"Well, I must confess, Controller," I concluded as he showed me out. "I'm a convert. But I don't expect you're looking for those."

"Good Heavens, no," he frowned. "That kind of thing went on when churches projected an image of their God or Jesus onto believers. They didn't give them choice, like nowadays."

I turned away and in the black emptiness of a switched-off video screen I caught sight of my own reflection. Vaguely I recalled something I'd read from the Bible in the antiquarian microfiche section of Herald Data Bank. It said, "God made man in his image." Or was it the other way round? □

The fear of big brother is abroad in the land

WHERE there is cable vision, the people perish, say the prophets of doom. They liken the pouring forth through the ether and via the cable of television programmes of every imaginable type, to the release into an estuary of toxic chemicals. The poisoning of minds is a cumulative business.

Others long for the new horizons, the flexibility and choice it will give them. They can even talk-back to the television. This alarms others who are unimpressed by being able to order their groceries down the tube and remember the TV-eye in Orwell's *1984* which spied on the populace as well as thundering propaganda messages at them. Fear of big brother is abroad in the land. High above us the celestial spheres of satellite communication look down upon us, observing any change in the weather, any reshuffle in the quiver of minutemen missiles in the United States' desert arsenal, any time Mrs McGinty fails to hang out her Tuesday wash.

In the beginning was television, then there was satellite and now there is cable and behold there are programmes throughout the land and there is plenteous choice. It was Marshall (the medium is the message)

McLuhan, the Canadian media guru, who said that the great revolutions in history had not been political or military, but the communication revolutions which altered the relationship between people in society. The Gutenberg Galaxy was the invention of the printing press which came just in time for the Reformation.

Printing press

If Martin Luther had had to preach his new doctrine round the pulpits of Germany, the new movement would have expired along with his horse and his larynx. But the printing press meant that each sermon could be distributed round the towns like an edition of the morning paper. It reached and influenced many more people. The world became much bigger and someone else discovered that it was round.

The quaint system known as wireless telegraphy then, telephones, radios and now television brought another revolution and the creation of a smaller world, the global village. It is a truism to say that we have not yet come to terms with it, or with the changes in relationships it has brought. Who is my neighbour? becomes a difficult question to answer for people who feel they know the characters in Dallas better than the folk on the floor beneath them in the multi-storey.

The dark side of this revolution is known as alienation, as the technical and penetration frontiers are pushed forward, so the flood of information surges and the fragile bonds between human beings are drowned in the torrent of words and images.

Gnawing vacuum

But like any revolution the new rulers are sometimes as tyrannous as the old ones. The stern rule of conformity to a static society is replaced by the gnawing vacuum that we have failed to conform to the new consumer society. The adverts scold us and cajole us and wheedle us and fawn us to keep up with the Joneses. The power of the message and the medium attracts like bees to a honey pot, those who crave power, particularly those who would be queen bee. Thus the schoolmasterish tone adopted by politicians who want the hive to be run according to their system.

Still others express horror about falling moral standards and foul language on television and see it as the agent of moral corruption of the young. Those who complain about such evil seduction usually do not have a great experience of the real world which existed long before TV and continued alongside it, sometimes being reflected by it, but always more horrific than TV. To some extent we are sheltered from the awfulness of reality by television. Over the piece it shows more beauty and riches than reality can master. Television does not show the squalid violence. Its violence excels in quality like the Kung Fu ballet of a film fight, but reality surpasses it in quantity.

Million views

Television is a window on the world with a difference. If you can afford the licence fee and a VCR, cable subscription and satellite dish, then you have a room with a million views. But beauty is in the eye of the beholder. The jaundiced eye sees not black and white but yellow and grey. It used to be that if you wished something to look white on television you had to paint it yellow. And as every greyhaired person knows by dint of experience, there is no black and white issue, only grey. All that is the conventional wisdom.

But the prophet says where there is no vision the people perish. Where there is television, there also must be vision, or the people perish. If therefore the real world is not shown perceptively and sensitively, there is both a loss of vision and of sensitive emotion. That is what is wrong with narcissistic chat shows which create, then devour, media personalities who have not achieved anything in the real world; or politics coverage which concentrates on the intra-party power struggles rather than the world to which the party hopes to appeal.

Like any tool, cable TV is what we make of it. It is a rope to hang ourselves, or a chain to link together diverse peoples. Dare I say it, it is like the Church. There is a branch in your local area, reflecting programmes from a satellite. You have competing systems and you have the freedom to switch them all off. You have the power to choose. But some people don't like having the responsibility of doing their own thinking—they let the Church or television do it for them. ☐

Losing out in the Battle of Wounded Knee

A Report from across the Atlantic . . .

LAW and gospel have traditionally been thought to be opposed to one another. This amazing country has thrown them into a new and unique relationship.

The "malpractice law suit" is no stranger to American courts and the hefty insurance premiums which doctors pay contribute to the high cost of medical care here. It also has the effect of making doctors jittery about stopping at road accidents which they come across. Should a victim die, they could find their good samaritan act has cost them a lot more than the penny which was paid to the Jericho–Jerusalem Motel. A malpractice law suit and legal fees could make a charitable gesture very costly indeed.

Medical malpractice law suits are now part of the American scene. What is new is clergy malpractice. It is easy to picture an inadequate anaesthetic, a slipped scalpel, an overlooked symptom, giving rise to dissatisfaction and a desire for redress. But a misinterpreted text, an inappropriate prayer, a hurried wedding ceremony; are these likely to result in damage to the soul?

Not quite. It has happened, in

California of all the likely places. It did not happen in some weird sect but in one of the largest and most prestigious Presbyterian churches in the Los Angeles area. The minister had been giving pastoral counselling to a youth with a disturbed relationship to his parents, particularly his mother. The youth moved in to stay temporarily at the manse but a crisis occurred and he committed suicide.

Three youths

His father persuaded the minister to conduct the funeral service without reference to the fact that he took his own life. The shame, the guilt, the remorse were weighing heavily upon the parents. But halfway through the service the minister spotted three youths who were also being counselled, each of whom could be a possible suicide. He prayed that none would be tempted to act wrongly as the deceased had done. Everyone then knew he had taken his life.

The father was furious that the minister had broken the agreement and brought a law suit for clergy malpractice, alleging incompetence that led to the death of his son.

At first the case failed because there was no category of clergy malpractice, but a Judge was found who soon put that right and the case is now proceeding to trial. A farce, you may say, since the vast majority of such cases result in an out of court settlement by a wealthy defendant (poor or uninsured persons are rarely the subject of such actions). Justice is not served and in this case the damages seem irrelevant.

I know of another case in Florida in which a 17-year-old boy bought booze from a Jax Liquor Store (a supermarket chain found throughout the state) in Tallahassee. It was against the law for him to do so and for the store to serve him. He got drunk, crashed his car and was permanently paralysed. He sued Jax Liquor Store for selling him the booze. An out of court settlement of $50,000 was paid since Jax did not want the publicity.

Moral crossroads

Yet although culpable for serving him, Jax cannot take responsibility for the three further moral crossroads through which the boy drove against the red lights—namely the decision to get drunk; the decision to drive in that state; and the decision to drive recklessly.

It is hardly just for the malefactor to blame his misdeeds on his parents, his teachers or his grocer for that matter. It is a shabby justification for bad behaviour to say that society or bad housing or education is responsible. But it shows real cunning to pursue damages in the law courts for shortfalls in one's own conduct.

Why do the lawyers entertain such absurdities, you may ask? The terrible truth is that many of them involved in damages or divorce cases in America are retained on a percentage basis. If they lose they get nothing. If they win they get a cut of the amount awarded. In other words it is a self-protection racket at which the American legal profession conspires.

They no doubt see it as an incentive

to do well for their client, and here in the free market lawyers solicit not only in court but in the newspapers, offering $95 divorces and other cut price rates. It is hardly an incentive to achieve justice or a catalyst to resolve cases speedily.

In Boston lawyers recently refought the Battle of Wounded Knee. A jogger who had brushed aside two evangelists from a religious cult had been pushed to the ground grazing his knee. The cult offered to pay his medical expenses of $200 and apologised. He sued for $100,000. He got $1000 and after paying his expert witnesses was left with a loss. However, the significant fact was that this incident took five years to come to court.

St Paul was surely right when he exhorted the early Christians to resolve their disputes among themselves without recourse to the court.☐

A down-to-earth case for tired feet

GOOD chiropodists are, apparently, thin on the ground. I have heard of older people who will literally walk the second mile despite weary feet aching with bunions, in order to visit a good chiropodist. Getting one's feet done has become part of the ritual of old age. But why only the elderly? My suggestion is that churches should institute the Sacrament of Feet Washing in its rightful and proper place.

After all there is greater Scriptural justification for such ritual than there is for infant baptism. Was the washing of the disciples' feet by Jesus not a heavily symbolic act, akin to the breaking of bread? It occurs in John's Gospel chapter 13 and is linked to the Passover, like communion. Jesus declares: "He who has bathed does not need to wash, except for his feet." Here is the reassurance which will be needed by those of you who have already begun to imagine a procession of sweaty limbs being uncovered in church to the discomfort of all. You will have had a bath before going along to the morning service of Chiropody, so the problem will not arise.

The woman who wept over the feet of Jesus in Luke chapter 7 and then proceeded to wipe his feet with her hair and anoint them with ointment, had her sins forgiven. Here then is an act that combines humility and repentance and stands along with baptism and communion as heavily symbolic ceremonies which require simple elements to carry them out. A bowl of warm water. A towel. Perhaps some sweet smelling ungent (what a lovely word that is). These are all that is needed for the sacrament of Chiropody.

All right, I am not being entirely serious. But I am certainly not being sacrilegious. We are altogether too frivolous towards feet and it is time that someone put their foot down. We cover them up and assume that when someone takes their socks off there will be a nasty smell. Quite apart from being the most down-to-earth thing about us, feet are a subtle source of sensuality. The art (therapy?) of Reflexology is founded on the principle that massaging the feet can affect the health of other parts of the body, a fact which acupuncture has known for a long time. It should therefore come as no surprise that gentle washing and drying of feet promote a feeling of wellbeing at the very least.

Just think of those winter evenings when you came home with feet like blocks of ice. A basin of hot water was prepared. A spoonful of yellow mustard was added and—oh joy of joys—as the feet were immersed a feeling of transcendent pleasure stole over you. Or just reverse the situation. It is a long hot summer's day. You have laboured up an unending hill with heavy feet which are swollen, sore and tired. A gurgling burn looms before you and in its cool streams you immerse your weary feet. Oooh, but it's lovely!

Herein perhaps lies the reason why feet have been so downgraded in our religious life. They are seductive sources of pleasure. Puritan and Calvinistic tradition would not approve of actually enjoying such a ceremony and no doubt someone would have pointed out that Ruth first caught Boaz's eye by uncovering his feet as he slept and lying alongside them. Clearly she knew the way to a man's heart was through his feet.

There are nearly as many mentions of feet in the Bible as there are of bread and yet feet remain unsung (except when Handel gives them their due with 'How beautiful are the feet . . .'). We even talk about armies marching on their stomachs, a typically perverse attempt to avoid giving credit to feet, upon which all armies march.

Feet also suffer from having a Latin derivation (pedes) which is rather similar to other classical roots. Etymologically, feet are thus associated with pedantry (vain pursuit of learning) or pederasty (sexual abuse of children). By using a Greek derivation, foot lovers could always describe themselves as podophiles. But at what price? They would soon be arrested for indulging in some pornographic practice when they were only wanting to wash one another's feet. It is indeed a hard slog for the podophile.

Let me again reassure those who suspect feet washing is some weird fetish, akin to the activities of those who achieve a thrill from handling women's shoes. Feet are the real thing. They do not possess the seductive allure of other parts of the female anatomy. You are not likely to see feet photos on page three, which has become synonymous with mammaries. Nor is there likely to be a change in fashion which results in feet being accorded the same status, much in the way that bottoms were favoured in the 'sixties, crotches in the 'seventies and ankles or wasp waists in Victorian times. Feet will remain wholesome.

The truth is that feet are an integral part of our senses as well as our support mechanism. We experience the world through our senses—tasting, smelling, touching, seeing, hearing. And we even extend that into our worship. There is the scent of flowers in the sanctuary or the whiff of incense. There is music to delight the ear and colour to capitvate the eye.

Why not touch to enthral the feet?

As St Paul reminds us, the body does not consist of one member but of many. "The eye cannot say to the hand, 'I have no need of you', nor the head to the feet, 'I have no need of you'." We vote with our feet. Why cannot we worship with them as well? □

Giving divinity a dog's chance

CHRISTMAS is about Incarnation, the Word becoming flesh. That is official—and orthodox. There are many sincere souls who find the idea of God becoming a human to be at best implausible, and at worst blasphemous. For example, followers of Islam would regard it as a blatant affront to the omnipotence of Allah/God that He should be confined within a mortal frame, yet they accord Jesus an important role as a prophet.

Most of us who are brought up in the Western Christian tradition take the divinity of Jesus for granted or regard it as a philosophical problem. Either we believe or we don't, and if we do, then we have various options open to us. Most of these options have been taken up in the days of the controversies over Christology.

The two natures theory says Jesus had two natures—one human, one divine. Another theory says that Jesus was only apparently human, another that he was adopted by God when he died, and still another that his body was human but his personality was divine. They all have shortcomings which I will not go into on this occasion, but which make them inappropriate models on which to slip the garments of orthodox doctrines of Atonement and the Trinity.

Some find it simpler to say that Jesus was human and leave it at that. A wise teacher, an inspiring prophet, a gifted healer—but a god? Never. This theory is probably held by more members of the mainstream Churches than they would care to admit. But this debate is never usually held in the open, and even if it is, the climate at Easter is usually more suitable.

At Christmas we are confronted with the face of a baby and it seems churlish to obstruct the tide of warmth and sentiment which flows out to descend on Bethlehem. There is a kind of miracle about the birth of any tiny baby which makes us suspend our critical stance. Any baby is divine and we do not grudge the Christ child that designation.

New life

But my most intractable theological problem is not Christological. Not being a parent, I have not had the experience of seeing the miracle of birth and feeling that curious way which mixes realisation of one's own mortality with the creation of new life. No, my problem is with a dog. My own dog. This creature (hereinafter referred to as the Blessed Dawg) possesses a divine expression of sadness, perception and sensitivity which many humans do not possess.

She sits in the passenger seat of the car on her haunches rather like a dowager duchess lacking the string of pearls, and glances about with curiosity. She reacts with affectionate enthusiasm that is loyal, genuine and utterly dependable. In short and in common with many other doting dog owners, I love the dog and the dog loves me.

The Blessed Dawg is, however, not divine. She has committed several sins, greed and gluttony being high on the list. But although large, she has the texture of a teddy bear and is coloured rather like one. She is a Rhodesian Ridgeback by breed and I resist the urgings of trendy idealogues who would rename these dogs which were used for lion hunting in East Africa. They want them to be called Zimbabwe Ridgbacks. Why does this inverted racialism not persecute Siamese kittens, I wonder? To me the BD is an RR among dogs.

But to my tale. For I appear to be going round in circles in answer to a question which has been worrying me for some time. It was brought home to me by the death of a friend's dog last week. He happens to be a minister and found himself amid considerable grief telling his young family that their dog had gone for a walk with Jesus. Now both he and I are aware that this is far from orthodox. The beasts of the field, pedigree or otherwise, were included by the Bible in the plan of salvation. Space there might have been in the Ark—but no dogs were allowed behind the pearly gates.

Contentious

Yet the nature of the beast is plain to see. It experiences love, loyalty. It knows the right and wrong which have been instilled into it and—a contentious assertion—sometimes it seems to know what is right or wrong even although it has no behavioural conditioning for that situation. Scoff if you like. But the concept of personality is as much fulfilled by a dog as by a human. That obviously does not extend to the levels of awareness which human consciousness exhibits, but where do you draw the line? The cruel truth is that some animals put some humans to shame.

A shrewd theologue said that personality has all to do with function. Give human values to the Blessed Dawg, and it will respond by living up to them. Thus I assist in the redemption of the dog if this be so. Just as I can rise above my baser instincts, so this is possible with the dog. But does the dog have a spirit? Could a dog survive death?

The question seems absurd until you realise that we know not in what manner the spirit survives. If it can, then the life force which drives the dog's personality might survive also. If believers can walk and talk with Jesus, why not with their beloved creatures? If the problem of how divine spirit became entangled with human flesh in the person of Jesus, is intractable—so too is the problem of how human spirit relates to a lowly creature. The theology of Incarnation and its theological problems does not stop at Bethlehem. So when people gather round the manger with wonder and puzzlement, I'm over in the corner looking at the cows. □

Responsibility of the Rupert Bear generation

INNOCENCE and a sense of responsibility. These were apparently the two qualities which Mr Alfred Bestall attributed to the character of Rupert the Bear which he drew for more than 30 years. Mr Bestall, who took over in 1935 from May Tourtel, Rupert's originator, died at the age of 93, but Rupert will live on in the minds of generations of children, some of them now drawing their pensions.

There is something cuddly and benign about a bear. Pandas, teddys, koalas—we love them all. Big softies like Mowgli, little honeypot bears like Pooh, and innocent and responsible bears like Rupert. I suppose if Rupert had not been a bear he might have been considered prissy, like Noddy. But he wasn't and he remains a beloved bear.

However, those two qualities—innocence and a sense of responsibility—do not appear to be so much in demand in children's stories if we are to believe a booklet published by the Evangelical Alliance. It preceded the book *Children at Risk* by David Porter (Kingsway).

"A barrage of children's books which include gratuitous violence, explicit sexual descriptions and ex-cursions into the twilight world of the occult ... a growing number of fantasy games which emphasise evil, horror and lawlessness." These are the allegations contained in the booklet, *Danger—Children at Play* (Evangelical Alliance, 186 Kennington Park Road, London SE11).

It proceeds to illustrate them with quotations from some of the Puffin children's books which have disturbed the authors. One, it claims, is illustrated with a mutilated doll pierced with needles, a decapitated man, a young nude girl on an altar. Another is concerned with the painful ways in which people can die, which include being eaten alive, dismembered and "un-souled".

It contains the sentence: "Looking down you see the bloody head of a harpoon protruding from your stomach. Your hands clutch at the gaping wound as you try to stop your entrails spilling into the slime of the sewer." Yet another features a quasi-black mass where a vampire creature "hands you the chalice and you have to drink. It is human blood, cursed in death's name".

That kind of blood-curdling prose makes some horror comics look positively decent. But I must admit that I read the booklet with some reserve. There have been instances recently of anti-porn campaigners over-gilding the lily. The shock/horror disclosure that children were watching video nasties in vast numbers was severely criticised when it was found that the research had undergone a little trimming with a chain-saw here and there.

There is also a kind of prurient obsession with filth among many

14

purity campaigners which I find distasteful. A minister friend of mine was once invited to meet Mrs Whitehouse and her cohorts at a Morningside home. The talk, in lurid detail, of filth and porn and how excruciatingly disgusting it all was, made my broadminded friend feel nauseated and he left.

I had a similar experience in the vestibule of the BBC with an interviewee from the Festival of Light who was declaiming the sins of magazines with open-crotch poses so loudly that I had to pretend I wasn't with him.

Recently, the Moral Majority campaigners in the US have targeted rock groups who are conveying occult messages in their songs and whose music, it is alleged, is the work of the devil. Again the terrible horrors which are claimed to be practised by these decadent punks are not always borne out when subjected to close scrutiny.

Notwithstanding these excesses of zeal, the Evangelical Alliance booklet does not appear to have gone over the top. It stresses the value of suggesting positive alternatives.

"Don't assume that any and every reference to the supernatural or any work of fantasy is harmful. Read Tolkien and C. S. Lewis. Consider how they used fantasy and other elements to convey truth."

Criticisms sent to the manufacturer/publisher will probably be listened to, it says, if based upon reasonable knowledge and an objective attitude. "Don't criticise games you have not seen. Apart from anything else, much written against Dungeons and Dragons, in particular, is very inaccur-

ate." You can't say much fairer than that.

Censorship is never a winning game. There is also a lot of humbug associated with campaigns to preserve the minds of children from pollution. The most absurd examples are those feminists who accuse Noddy of being sexist, or the golliwog on the marmalade pot of being racist. However, in both these instances the commercial pressure of the campaigning groups has been enough to effect change. The Evangelical Alliance is canny in hoping it can win similar victories by persuading publishers that it is in their commercial interest to avoid offending decent consumers.

But—ugly thought. What if in our freemarket country (where Colonel Gaddafi could, theoretically, buy as many shares in a helicopter company as he liked), enough people do not care what children buy or read? Could we have a board game called The Yorkshire Ripper where you throw dice to travel around the red-light areas of Yorkshire picking up points for prostitutes encountered on the way? Could we substitute a Dennis Nilsen version of Treasure Hunt in which you have to guess where he's buried the bodies? It's disgusting—but it's possible.

It is simply the factual equivalent of some of the fictional tales on sale to children today. The EA booklet cites Scream magazine, published by IPC, as presenting evil as part of everyday life instead of an intrusion into life which must be resisted in the way of the traditional comics.

There have always been creepy-crawly stories, which are part of learning that life is not all teddy bears and roses. But there are degrees of disgustingness. Loving portrayal in vivid art form all that is vile in human behaviour, or the presentation of occult powers as real and exciting, are far from balanced. Should we wonder that they might influence some children to think that the real world is all like that?

We, of the Rupert Bear generations, may not have retained our innocence but we surely have a duty to keep a sense of responsibility to the next generation. ☐

Down the theological black hole

THE bottom has dropped out of morality, according to Lord Hailsham, who added that the "last few months have been particularly difficult to bear." Bear might be an appropriate metaphor for the former Lord Chancellor himself. He is capable of avuncular charm, wheezy laughter and mischievous wit as well as grizzly ferocity and stick-in-the-mud reactionary attitudes and walking-stick-in-the-hand swashbuckling. In short, he is not dull but often comes across as one of those who favour a return to "Victorian values".

Such a description is not at once clear. Victorian values might include

slavery, children down the mines and chimney sweeps up the stack, as well as gin parlours and asylums. Clearly this is not what Lord Hailsham wants. He says he agrees with Mr Tebbit that many of the evil deeds of recent years which have seen child murders and terrorism of a particularly disgusting type, cannot be answered by "mere questions of policing, penal treatment or sentencing policy and cannot either be justified or explained by talking of urban deprivation and unemployment."

With this I also agree. However, it is hardly an answer. It is more of a denial of another answer, the facile solution to our present problems which calls for greater sums to be spent on social services in order to provide a world free from crime, disease and ignorance.

How Utopian and how irrelevant this seems when a microscope is taken to social problems and they show up as being caused by individuals, some of whom are rich and some of whom are poor. Some are kind, some callous. Some are selfish, some are caring. Here the Tebbit school of thought seems to be saying, "It is up to the individual to build a new world through his own efforts." This too is surely Utopian and completely ignores the collective side of humanity.

Both the welfare socialists and the individualistic Tories are right as well as wrong in their analysis. Both would cost us dear with their simplistic solutions. One would have us dismantle the wealth generated by capitalism on the one hand and at the same time ask us to increase spending on areas of need. The other would allow the smart to inherit the Earth (plus a legacy from their wealthy parents) and console us with the exhortation to work harder if we want more, which goes down like a glass of sand in the unemployment deserts.

It is tempting to consider the real debate in society to be this one, the one they have at Westminster. It has all the cut and thrust of an ideological conflict. It has the smell of glamour and the roar of a crowd (even if this occasionally drowns out Mr Tebbit's speeches). It even has hooliganism and violence and so must run football very close to being an alternative religion. So with football and politics as the bread and circuses of our decadent empire—whither religion?

That is the problem. Even the churches, in making reports about Gartcosh, teachers' pay, inner-city deprivation or whatever, are drawn into this political debate and inevitably they feel in order to be relevant they must offer political and practical solutions. That is where I believe they are making a mistake and where they are open to expose their ignorance and naivete.

Mr Tebbit is sometimes portrayed as a pantomime villain when he roughs up the clerics who venture to assume the prerogative in the political sphere. Give me that brutal honesty any day to the sleazy condecension of some of his colleagues in telling the well-intentioned churchmen to mind their own business.

The fact is that the business of the politicians is distinct and different from the business of the churches. Let no one kid us into treating politicians as prophets whom we elevate and then abuse and then stone to death.

They have enough problems avoiding the stones they are throwing among themselves to be dealt such an additional blow. So do not let us be surprised when they fail to deliver the goods from their two-cornered debate.

There is another dimension to the decadence of Britain and the Western world. It is to do with souls, not bodies politic. Just as there is a material dimension there is a spiritual dimension. And the Earthly city is not equivalent to the Heavenly city. But, just as in politics there is a clash of ideas between global and individual philosophies, in religion there is the dichotomy between the group soul and the individual. Where I think the problem lies is that the Victorian age was one which stressed personal salvation and the individual soul. Now there is little or nothing left of that theology among Church leaders, it being mainly the prerogative of evangelical back benchers. But instead of embracing the group soul (Jung's Collective unconscious) the inevitable consequence of the backlash into demythologising has been to surrender this concept to the Greenpeace/Aquarian/New Age wholemeal-sandals people.

The Church is then left with no alternative but to see salvation in Earthly terms since it has abandoned faith in a collective spiritual kingdom and relies on a shaky humanist spirituality.

What we are seeing is not churchmen meddling in politics but following through the logic of their theology which Professor T. F. Torrance has dubbed "a radical disjunction between faith and reason."

He and I may be strange companions in the same lobby but I am certain he has put his finger on an error which condemns many modern Church leaders to disappear down a theological black hole.

On the one hand they have abandoned the pre-Copernican world and pre-Darwinian attitudes to the Bible, but they have still not discovered the real centre of the spiritual universe. Assuming it to be out there somewhere they have joined forces with the Utopians and Marxists and missed the fact that the spiritual galaxy for which they are searching is like the Milky Way. We are in it and part of it and it is all around us. □

Saints who should be seen as well as heard about

WHEN a headless body dramatically floated from the West of England to descend at Clapham by London amid a throng of witnesses and a pair of Cardinals, it was no miracle, no ghostly occurrence. It was the somewhat ghoulish climax to the celebration of St Oliver Plunkett Day when a helicopter brought the 300-year-old body from its resting place. (The head is in Drogheda in Eire). Oliver Plunkett was an Irish Jesuit executed for treason on July 1, 1681 and canonised five years ago.

His original crime was allegedly that he was plotting to bring 20,000 French soldiers into Ireland and trying to raise a further army by levying a charge on the poverty stricken clergy of Ireland among whom he was doing mighty works in reviving the Catholic faith. However well suited he might seem to become the patron saint of the IRA, the cap does not fit. For the evidence was perjured and by bringing a charge of treason in an English court, a conviction was secured. The Judge declared that the foundation to this treason was setting up a false religion.

We are more tolerant these days. But there are some who would say that there is now a contemporary form of false religion (idolatry and superstition if you prefer) in the veneration of such characters and their elevation to sainthood. Those who think this way were not impressed when the Scots counterpart of Plunkett, St John Ogilvie, was canonised in 1976. Ogilvie had been executed for treason, but his real crime was refusing to acknowledge the king's dominion in matters spiritual.

Roll up yonder

Both saints were subjected to the elaborate canonisation procedure before their names were added to the roll up yonder, and down yonder in the Vatican.

The ceremony in itself was solemn by which St John Ogilvie was created until the shaky voice of Pope Paul announced to the assembled thousands of pilgrims in St Peter's that the moment had arrived. As an outside observer I was startled by the response — a roar that would have drowned even the Parkhead faithful saluting their team captain clutching the Scottish Cup. The organ played. Holy chaos reigned for a few moments while all heaven was let loose. St Peter had opened the pearly gates and St John Ogilvie had prodded home the penalty. One-nil to the Jesuits!

That's how it seemed to the mystified outsider. Less amused spectators might have worried that the whole practice was superstitious.

Others might quarrel on theological grounds that the litany of the saints amounts to a cult of the dead, or ancestor worship. There is the further objection that Christian orthodoxy (be it Catholic or Protestant) teaches that the Son has sole access to the Father within the Holy Trinity and that He is the sole advocate before the throne of Judgment. To introduce canonised solicitors into the Supreme Court of the universe is to disrupt this system. It means that man can influence the events of heaven. This destroys the supremacy of God. Dial a Saint equals cheap man-made grace, say the objectors.

This picture is, however, a caricature of Roman Catholic teaching on the subject, although unfortunately not always a caricature of Catholic practice. The veneration of saints has a long history dating back to the early martyrs (meaning witnesses). These were people who showed courage, faith, and were an example to all by making the supreme sacrifice. Hence they were held out as examples. Miracles were attributed to some saints and special powers to others.

League system

All 'miracles' were put to exacting test, with the 'Devil's Advocate' trying to prove them false.

Of course many of the less respectable saints remained on the calendar, their only usefulness being the excuse for a holiday or a village carnival. In 1969 the calendar was revised so that greater emphasis could be given to the major festivals of the Christian year. The number of saints was pruned, including a few Popes; and a three league system introduced for the feast days of saints. Premier League is for solemnities. First Division is reserved for such as apostles, at the rate of two or three per month. Second Division is for 'memories'—commemorations which are either obligatory or optional. As well as tidying up the whole system, it re-affirms that the doctrine of saints has a place, but not the central place, in Catholic piety.

Why should Protestants grudge the Roman Catholics their saints? They are a reminder that faith speaks of life that is unbroken by death. Talking to saints as if they were there, is surely nothing but a mark of faith. Yet it is worth reminding Catholics that when Paul in the New Testament refers to the saints (*hagioi*) he means the church people who are alive at that time. The saints or 'holy ones' should be seen as well as heard about. They are part of the church visible as well as invisible.

A saint is not prayed to. He or she is remembered in prayer and asked to in turn pray for the person's desired object. The place of Christ as the agent of intercession is not eroded. To my mind the most powerful argument for having saints is that they are such a diverse bunch that among them will be at least one person that even the most eccentric believer can identify with.

Lowly born or high born there is a saint for you. Even if you're awkward and want a Japanese aristocrat with no left ear, then you cannot beat the Celestial store at the Vatican. They can offer you St Miki and Companions (died 1597). And they all come with a seal of approval.   □

Mirror in which we see image of God

THE best sermon I have so far heard was on the subject of 'ontological anxiety'. Before some of you scoff at the obscurity of such a subject, let me tell you what the preacher meant (or rather what I think the preacher meant) by it. He was saying that the very fact of being alive inevitably leads us to experience doubts, fears, anxiety. Not only are these perfectly natural consequences of human consciousness, but they are utterly necessary to live a life of any depth whatsoever.

The bland and the placid may seem to sail through life but they are either living a superficial existence or else, like the rest of us, they experience the long shadow of despair. Perhaps some of them are good at putting on a face,

saving the grim reality for private moments. There are others less admirable, who can banter away with colleagues and friends but who save their bile of resentment for their spouse or family. Restless and unwound at home, their tongue lashes around venting their self-doubt and guilt on others.

The less articulate lash out in more phiysical ways. Mean and vile and sad. It is the portrait of a caged animal sniffing the air in search of a scent of meaning in life. It is ontological anxiety minus hope, faith, and love.

Let us suppose that it was somehow possible to banish the feelings which give rise to such ugly behaviour in human beings. Peace would reign in everyone's mind. Placidly we would go amid the strife of modern life. The Garden of Eden would have returned, but let us remember what it entailed. Prior to eating of the fruit of the tree of knowledge of good and evil, Adam and Eve were not troubled by ontological anxiety. There were no nasty choices to be made between different courses of action. Free to roam, there was a free market in morality and it didn't matter what choice was made, everything continued to end happily.

No winners but no losers either. It sounds like a Sunday School party. And it is just as horrifying an idea to contemplate being walled into such a Paradise Garden as being condemned to spend eternity playing games with balloons which never burst, receiving presents from Santa without wondering how they were paid for, being organised into teams with leaders chosen arbitrarily from among us, or eating a permanent celestial buffet of ice cream and salmon sandwiches. Without struggle there can be no progress, and struggle presupposes winners and losers. The act of participation arouses the spiritual adrenalin of anxiety.

Bereft of hope

So far so realistic. But sometimes it gets pretty depressing doesn't it? The black dog of melancholy follows the footsteps of any pilgrim. Because no Sunday School teacher is there to see that everyone gets a prize, that no one cheats or that no one is left lonely and out in the cold, there will be casualties. Bereft of hope, unable to find faith and unloved, some such people seek an end to their misery in suicide. I have never been able to subscribe to the extreme schools of thought which see this either as a sin or as an act of brave defiance. Surely it is a poignant reminder of the capacity of the human being to suffer mental anguish. It is when ontological anxiety has surpassed fear and become terror.

It is curiously not in January when the climate is at its most bleak and icy that suicides peak. It is just as the nights are getting lighter when the sights of spring are just beginning to show. Is there something significant in this, that the blackbird scolding through the bonny banks makes a heart that is weary and full of care, well up inside with pain? Is it coincidence that the most satisfying music is sad? I do not believe it is. Nor do I believe that the conclusion to be drawn from all this is that life is a miserable business.

Which brings me back to the sermon with which I started. It was about the inevitability of anxiety, yet its effect on me was not palliative, I was not mildly reassured. I was invigorated and felt seven feet tall going out of the church. If not the glory, the credit belongs to Murdo Ewen MacDonald, who was the preacher. The fact I have remembered its message after 12 years is a testimony to its effectiveness.

What was perhaps so satisfying about the sermon was that it was able to turn an apparently negative quality into a positive asset. The hallmark of the Christian faith is that it turns an apparent defeat into a victory. The rejection of a loving, caring being by a cruel world becomes a proof of God's love and a demonstration of its indestructibility. Such a story could be viewed cynically as making a virtue out of necessity and that is indeed what it does do. It is necessary to experience anxiety, pain, and death because we are alive. The tremendous sense of liberation is in seeing this not as an obstacle to faith, a rock of doubt which blocks progress, but as a part of the essence of life itself.

Without such a sense of pain we would be anaesthetised to the plight of others. If we did not have this sense, we would view those suicides as silly neurotics who were either mad or stupid. Only by sharing anxiety do we participate in a meaningful existence.

Not only does that provide a common bond among humanity to evolve spiritually, but it gives an insight into the nature of a God who often reveals Himself in paradox. The expression 'pain of love' is paradoxical. Yet it encapsulates the central themes of the Christian faith. To be vulnerable to pain and love at one and the same time is to be close to the ground of our very being. It is to be seven feet tall and yet to have one's feet on the earth which the creator made. It is to be fully human and yet to know that the Garden of Eden man is the creature of clay feet. Anxiety is the mirror in which we see the image of God. ☐

Ultimate sex movie

FILMS about the human sex act are rather like books on the same subject. They range from the pornographic to the didactic style of Open University programmes. In trying to describe the mechanics of something which is more emotional than clinical, more sensual than physiological, they occasionally range into the ridiculous, but could almost never be described as sublime.

There are, of course, many works of 'art' which portray this area of human activity. Have not paintings of nudes been presented as such? And was not *Lady Chatterley's Lover* defended on the grounds that it was a work of literary genius? However, I cannot get excited by them (and that applies to the passion they generate in a sexual as well as a moralistic sense) and would certainly not ever describe them as sublime.

But the Swedish film-maker Gunnar Nilsson has produced a science film which is pure art. It is both sublime and artistic and combines the secrets of the laboratory with arcane mysteries of creative talent and, of all things, is a documentary about how human reproduction takes place. It is the ultimate sex movie.

A tiny lens was able to penetrate the womb, then the fallopian tubes, then the ovary itself. There the microscopic ovum was revealed and followed as it started its monthly journey to await possible fertilisation. But as the complex and delicate process unravelled, with hormones triggered off like the unlocking of a set of combination locks in a vast bank vault, it emerged how unlike a precious gem the ovum is.

Many are wasted and when the magic lens peeped into the male sex organs, the wastage increased a millionfold. Deformed sperms, de-energised sperms and sperms deterred by the acid environment of the womb, were catalogued so that when the camera followed the successful ones on their journey it seemed a miracle that any got to their destination at all.

Then the moment of conception itself. Life created before the camera's eye. Springing up microscopically on the double helices to create that most controversial of creatures— the human embryo.

To those like me whose education concentrated on the physical rather than the biological sciences, the Nilsson film was a revelation. Here was clear exposition of the biology involved. Here was a film akin to the first pictures from the moon but with a difference. The barren moonrock and dust cannot evolve into anything whereas the tiny cartwheel of molecules becomes a foetus, then a baby, then a full human being. As the film rolled, ignorance for me became awe.

Precious quality

Whether the timing of this programme was influenced by the current debate on embryo research, I do not know. But it helped me to gain a deeper appreciation of what is involved. First there is the realisation that Nature allows for wastage and a random element. It also allows a helping and an inhibiting hand, or enzyme, to stop and start the processes. Should a higher form of awareness decide to tip the balance here or there (perhaps by embryo implantation) or put it on ice (as in frozen embyros) so that knowledge can be gained which will enable future embryos to prosper healthily, then it will not be acting contrary to what Nature itself does by trial and error and evolution.

To say otherwise is to give Nature a status as divine revelation which the victims of congenital diseases would not thank you for. "We've always done it this way" is as daft an excuse for an industrial manufacturing process which has become fossilised as it is for saying that fossils have a life of their own. In other words, watching the film persuaded me that despite the intricacy of the life-producing process, it is not wrong to think of helping it along in certain ways. Thus I am not in principle against the idea of research into embryos.

However, the second compelling point which struck me in watching the film was a realisation that this was like watching a film of a milk bottling plant. It was not mechanical but mystical. The embryo travels to become an adult in an ubroken line, which leads many to say that it is equivalent to a human life in moral status.

Of course, it would not get there without help. Without the midwife, the mother, the sustaining hand, the child would spoil. They too are part of the Nature which brings life into being. The whole moral right does not therefore repose in the embryo or the foetus but in the parent and in the medical personnel acting on behalf of society into which such a child would be born. It is not as simple as saying an embryo has a value equal to one human life which it is entitled to cash in.

To say this is not to belittle the sincere concern shown by many religious people in the debate over embryo research. They are being consistent with their own theological position. They bear witness to the precious quality of the embryo and the birth process. But shouting murder at those who are trying their best to maintain quality of life from another standpoint is neither appropriate, nor likely to produce a healthy outcome for society.

The Roman Catholic Church must take a great deal of credit for consistently arguing the 'pro-life' case. That is why it is sad to see so much bitter polemic springing out of sincere concern. But to argue that an embryo is sacred is different from saying that a sperm is sacred. That is what the illogical anti-contraception stance of the Roman Catholic Church is in effect saying—and as that film so vividly illustrated that would mean a mini-genocide going on inside every male every minute.

The Irish Government may some day allow non-Catholics, and Catholics too, to buy contraceptives in Eire. To hold an anti-contraceptive view is one thing, but to enshrine it in the law of the land is another. Those who have denounced the pro-contraceptionists so bitterly should remember their own dictums, that Protestants—like embryos—ought to have rights too. □

Religion with the ring of truth

TO most people philosophy is a phunny business. To judge by appearances Nietzsche was a loony who went round market places declaring God to be dead and eventually was declared mad (although from his earlier work *Zarathustra* the matter was never in doubt). Wittgenstein was a whizzkid who wanted to be an aviator and ended up teaching philosophy at Cambridge from a green deck chair. The present Dean of Emmanuel College Cambridge, Revd Don Cupitt, concluded in his *Sea of Faith* TV series (and book) that these two thinkers must represent what has happened to religious thinking in the last 100 years.

The former used poetic and dramatic style to convey the literally awful realisation that the more science was able to discover about the machinery by which the world goes round, the more we become alone

within it. God is then banished from our reality. Only man's will to triumph over life survives, making the world a human jungle in which religion is at best evolutionary humanism.

Wittgenstein, according to Don, explored the way we use language to substitute for reality. It does not describe reality nor is it sufficent in itself, but applied to religion it means that nothing is true. Creeds are only notices pointing in the direction in which deep down feelings and beliefs are taking us. No objective reality means no certainties and that means agnosticism.

At first sight this is another version of the doom and gloom story. Trendy clerics selling out the faith of their fathers and sending away flocks with empty bellies. But the charge of a conspiracy among philosophers and theologians to take away the toys and joys of faith will not stick. Thinkers, like the aforementioned, gained status because they suggest answers that have the ring of truth. The answers, the systems of thought, are the bell—not its ring.

The two can become confused. Philosophers point out the existence of God cannot be proved and terms like good or love cannot be defined in a way that has real independent existence outwith our wishful thinking. But that is another way of saying the ring cannot be seen, measured, touched or heard by picking up the bell and sniffing it, weighing it and subjecting it to chemical analysis.

We can imagine the bell without imagining its ring. We can imagine a ring. But if we only know the bell according to those systems we call logic or science, then we can only talk about bells. Some philosophers know a lot about bells and think that everyone who hears ringing noises in their ears must have bats in the belfry.

But we mustn't blame philosophers if they tell it as they see it with the aid of their philosophical telescopes and microscopes. It is only if theologians go on using the old equipment (sun goes round earth etcetera) that they fall out with the philosophers and scientists. God as an old man with a beard pulling strings up in the sky is doomed forever to be invisible and impossible. But that is not the point.

This is not a battle between clever intellectuals and poor, simple people who believe what the churches tell them. Their philosophers have liberated non-intellectuals by declaring faith to be independent of cleverness and education and social style. It does not need to be taught like mathematics or French. It is within the grasp of the humblest creature. Why then is there so little of it in our doom-laden age?

Philosophy is now esoteric. It is the stuff of ivory towers and only clever boys and girls are expected to reflect upon its themes. I remember once having a passion to read and argue endlessly on such topics. I didn't solve them but thinking about them was good exercise. Jogging the mind. Now I've gone lazy but I still have enough gumption to realise the breakthrough is not going to be intellectual but spiritual.

The Nobel prize for religion (God forbid it should ever be invented) will not go to a theologian, or like the peace prize be passed round to whoever fits the political needs of the moment (with all due respect to Bishop Tutu and not much to Mr Begin). It will go more probably to an unknown office cleaner whose life is as anonymous as a flower but just as perfect or beautiful. For breakthroughs in religion are made by individuals who make sense of the mystery of existence not in their minds but in their hearts.

They may do it with the help of the symbols of the church, or the language of the Bible in the orthodox way. But there is nothing logical to prevent them finding it in Eastern religions or in hill-walking. Feelings, experiencing the transcendent, the numinous, the religious dimension— whatever you choose to call it—can like bells come in many sizes and sorts.

Like the ring of the bell there is an authentic note which differentiates these sentiments from emotionalism or sentimentality. They require nurturing, working at. But it can be done inside the head. You don't have to go anywhere to study. There is no capital city for pilgrims, no head office in a worldwide church, no head priest to tell you what teachings you must follow.

That is where the real revolution comes in the days following Wittgenstein. It cuts out the middleman. Luther, who put the Bible in the hands of the people and introduced the priesthood of all believers in the previous great spiritual revolution, will be succeeded by a system which cuts out the need for a church except for those who want it.

The present churches are right to be concerned that many do not give themselves the opportunity to grow in

25

any faith because apathy and false gods have moved into the vacuum that exists instead of a soul. The ground on which the church fights the battle will be crucial. If they fight over philosophy or science they will inevitably lose. If they go into the market place where they can command personal insight of a Christian way of life then they will move with the times. □

Finding the words for ears of children

"YOU always get something to take away with you in the Children's Address." I have often heard this said as a last-ditch attempt by adults to find consolation or uplift from a dreich church service or one in which the sermon was the dominant factor and was long-winded or incomprehensible or both.

This takeaway sermonette is usually tucked away after the opening prayer and before the second hymn, during which the children leave church (in the months when Sunday School is in session). In the summer months when there is no Sunday School there are sometimes no children. The minister is then faced with the task of keeking to see during that prayer whether there are enough potential listeners to justify proceedings with his prepared material.

For good children's addresses are more precious than rare ointment and there is no sense in casting piglet pearls to adult swine. At least that will be the attitude of the minister who has scrabbled around (perhaps even ringing up a colleague on the Saturday night) in a desperate search for that elusive thing, the good children's address. However, should he look round, decide that there are no children and omit the address, there will be dark mutterings: "He missed oot the children's address. . . ."

Chance to frolic

The tactics for this sermon for all the family vary considerably. Some ministers deliver a shorter version of an adult sermon. Others freak out and enjoy the chance to frolic. So out come the glove puppets, the posters and the toys which can be used to illustrate the point. Anthing goes, and the more he goes down-market the more they love it. Warm smiles play over the faces of the grannies as the meenister cavorts. His critics even smile in anticipation of a rhetorical question meeting with a devastating reply. Out of the mouths of babes . . . comes many a minister's comeuppance.

There are some ministers who eschew the delights of the children's address. The more pompous argue that it destroys the dignity of the service. The more thoughtful among them point out that although many parts of the service may be over the heads of the kids, it is nevertheless directed at all worshippers and no part of the service ought to be segregated from another. It is liturgically unsound, they might say, to use

26

worship as instruction. Of course this all depends on your opinions or your taste, factors which play a large part in religious observance.

Playing to the gallery

Some ministers perhaps keep it on because they feel that it caters for a section of the adult church with whom they are unwilling to compromise in the sermon. This would be quite acceptable if the discipline of expressing their message in simple terms were followed through. But so often the challenge is not met and the result is a wishy-washy moral parable. "So you see, children, the moral of the story is that if you are good then God will be pleased. . . ."

Worse is the sacrifice of theological integrity for the sake of playing to the gallery. The common fault of children's stories is that they grab the attention with some device, amuse thoroughly, but end up answering no questions. What is the good of having Rod Hull's Emu in the pulpit if he buries his head in the theological sands.

You may think that I am too harsh and write with lack of sympathy for the children, expecting them to struggle with concepts which cause greater minds a great deal of thought. But the point is that the mind of a child is often capable of a greater grasp of the complexity of a theological problem than an adult. Addressing questions to a class of primary school children in a rural school at the time of the Passover, I asked them about places in the Bible where there were sheep. We read the story of the Passover in Egypt. I mentioned that Jesus was sometimes called the Lamb of God. They put the ideas together and I suddenly became aware that they were teaching me about substitutionary atonement.

Meaningless

Of course, children lose that intuitive wisdom. They become schooled in that illogical negatism sometimes known as Logical Positivism, which says that statements about the world are either provable by observation or are capable of being deduced from facts supplied by reason or logic. Since statements like "God is Love" fall into neither category they are held to be meaningless. "Make love not war" is held to be meaningless except that it is a convenient mutual treaty by which humanity favours co-operation and survival, rather than dangerous destruction. Moral statements therefore lack any force except pragmatic pay-off. But the original premise that all statements are either empirical or analytical is itself in neither of these categories. The atheist house is built on sand.

But we have been brought up to respect these intellectual tools so much that they supplant the innocent insight of a child. One day a child came home from Sunday School declaring that he had just been hearing about how Moses crossed the Red Sea with tanks and Bailey bridges. Soldiers had parachuted across, but mortar fire had seen them off. When his father remonstrated with him and refused to believe that the respectable staff of the Sunday School had put any such nonsense in his head, the wee boy protested: "But if I told you what we did learn about Moses and the Red Sea, you'd never believe me." □

A promise is a promise—especially on a Sunday

REMEMBER the Sabbath day to keep it holy. The words of the Fourth Commandment are uncompromising and it's assumed that so also are those who believe in keeping the Sabbath. They are characterised by the woman who clucked her disapproval to a minister of my acquaintance about an instance of Sabbath breaking. "But Jesus did acts of kindness on the Sabbath," he replied, thinking to meet her objection on Biblical grounds. "Aye," she said undeterred, "and He ought to have known better."

Such puritanical zeal is associated with the Sabbath-keeping habits of that last stronghold of the pure gospel in the Western Isles, where bacon lies cold on the plates in the digs of even tax-dodging landladies on a Sabbath morn. Sizzle and aroma do not profane the all-pervading stillness.

No doubt there are a few places where Stornoway citizens get drunk at Sunday lunchtime, indeed, there are quite a few of them, but their doors are shut to the public; sin goes private on the Sabbath for it is public morality which counts in Sabbath observance.

Dirty linen, or even the freshly laundered variety, is not hung out to dry.

No surprise

That is the way many of us view the attitude of the Lord's Day Observance Society. Our horizons are broader, we think, basking in liberality and charity. It comes as no surprise to us that the LDOS has managed in recent years to attract packed houses for public meetings to oppose Sunday working at the construction site at Arnish Point near Stornaway and for the campaign against Sunday sailings to the Western Isles by Cal-Mac.

The people of Lewis do not always present a sympathetic profile but in this case they had my sympathy and for two reasons. The first is that the land around the Arnish site was owned by the Stornoway Trust, an elected body who received an undertaking from the subsidiary of Olsen Shipping when they took over the site, that only essential maintenance would be carried out on Sundays. Olsens said that Sunday working would be essential to keep the yard open. The Trust took out an interdict. After all, a promise is a promise, is a promise.

It would appear that in this moral stance they were backed by public opinion. Before you dismiss that as a cultural aberration of Gaeldom, consider my second reason. The Western Isles has one of the highest unemployment levels in Britain. If overtime was indeed needed, so perhaps was work-sharing, a modern idea which tries to spread the dignity of jobs around.

Day of rest

If you can share a job when all around are losing theirs, not only are you a big man, but an unselfish one. Indeed the whole issue of Sabbath observance could be set for a return to fashion. Increased leisure opportunities have meant that people can take their leisure during the week and leave Sunday as a day of rest.

Think of the peace which would prevail if traffic stopped, planes ceased to roar overhead, and the ceaseless consumer buzz were silent. People might read, or even talk to one another. They might rediscover the space between words and the gulf between them and those with whom they live. Oh yes, they might want to worship God but let's take one step at a time. If modern man is to be persuaded, it will be on pragmatic grounds. "Ecologically, sociologically, physiologically, psychologically—you know it makes sense!"

Bird song

Put like that it seems less like a divine commandment and more a TV ad for increased leisure. Indeed, it was watching television recently that I came to the conclusion that what the Lord's Day Observance Society needs is a good PR man. He could evangelise us disguised as a doctor who wants us to rest our bodies, an environmentalist who wants us to slow down, or as a psychiatrist telling us we will be less neurotic if we put our feet up and listen to the bird song for one day a week.

Cuckoo? Don't we have enough public holidays without adding to them? Yes, but the trouble is they are unco-ordinated. May Day is celebrated absurdly in different parts of Cosla's domain on different days. Easter is when Chitty Chitty Bang Bang is shown on television and when schoolchildren get a holiday—except when the educational authorities do not have their Easter holidays at Easter.

Keeping the Sabbath was originally one of the Ten Commandments because it kept aside time to honour the Creater. Today's consumers do not keep the Sabbath, but keep their shops open and anything else they can lay their hands on. The people of Lewis keep the Sabbath and their honour. □

The case for seeing through a glass darkly

CHARLES DARWIN opened a can of worms which have been crawling their way up the evolutionary ladder of history ever since. The Great Debate of Victorian times was whether man evolved from the monkeys, as Darwin's theory suggested, or whether he was created as part of the six-day week being worked by the Almighty in Genesis. As in any full-blown controversy, these polarised positions were the ones taken up by most contributors to the fight.

Fifty-six years ago in Tennessee a teacher named Charles Scopes was convicted in a court case of teaching evolution to his pupils. The issue is never far beneath the surface in the buckle of the Bible Belt in Little Rock, Arkansas. The American Civil Liberties Union brought a case against the State, attempting to undo a new State law which requires that the creation theory be balanced alongside the theory of evolution in schools. I have put it like that because the law does not mention God and concentrates on 'balance' rather than 'equal time' as some papers have reported.

What made the issue especially controversial is that the American Constitution requires that Church and State be completely separate, and most Americans, churches included, accept that this means no religion must be taught in schools.

The new law, they argued, is an infringement of this principle. Nonsense, said the Fundamentalists, it is the Civil Liberties people who are being illiberal and intolerant by presenting evolution as fact when it is only a theory. Federal Judge William Overton ruled in favour of the petitioners that the new law was unconstitutional. (Some 15 other states where the Moral Majority are by no means the silent majority, had hoped to pass similar laws, but it is now assumed that the case will go to appeal and eventually reach the Supreme Court).

Hot gospel

It is not simply a legal issue or even a theological one. It is a scientific issue. All three disciplines were represented in the court and they produced some highly unlikely permutations. Theological hawks and doves lay down with scientific lions and legal lambs. There were demonstrators in monkey suits and even a man in a devil costume who served chilli to spectators. Hot gospel?

Such razzmatazz is not conducive to a proper spirit of inquiry. My prize for the most colourful quote goes to the scientist who said that the likelihood of humans having come about as the result of evolution was the same as a tornado in a scrapyard having accidentally assembled a Jumbo jet. He is a colleague of the cosmologist Sir Fred Hoyle who espoused the 'steady-state' theory of the creation of the universe in the 'fifties. Hoyle may seem to be an unlikely bedfellow with the Bible-believers, but his stated objection to the Civil Liberties Union case is that they may be imposing a theory on the schoolchildren of Arkansas which is scientifically wrong. The real question is not whether the Book of Genesis has it right (most modern theologians read it as a poetic account) but whether evolution is correct.

Hoyle writes: "My own recent work has caused me to doubt, not that evolution takes place, but that it takes place according to the usual theory of natural selection operating on randomly generated mutations. What I find is that far too often the facts suggest a reversal of the expected relation of cause to effect, the cart comes too often before the horse."

The scientist who hangs on to yesterday's theory as if it were eternal truth is liable to be dumped on the flat earth—where he belongs. The proper scientist sees reality through a glass darkly—and believeth all facts, heareth all facts and seeth all facts, but still has to reckon with the fact that he is part of the experiment and may be seeing the reflection of his own opinions. The litmus test between the great mind and the clever mind is that the former is always conscious of how little he knows, and the latter of how much he knows.

Two methods

Those principles could well be applied to theology, which has been called the queen of the sciences. It can be approached in two ways. The first is a humble spirit of inquiry, trying to fit the observed facts and experiences of life into a pattern of theory known as doctrine. The other way of practising theological science is to start with a system of dogmatic theology and find it confirmed in the experience of life.

The former will never have the ring of eternal truth and will always have a suspicion of temporary or symbolic truth about it. The latter will end by confirming or rejecting the original theory, but humans, being what they are, will usually manage to prove themselves right and join some kind of inquisition to make sure everyone else is proved right too.

That is why I side with the scientists and the Fundamentalists of Arkansas against the fake liberals. The trouble usually arises when a theological theory is claimed to be a concrete principle (a disease which also afflicts sociologists and psychologists) or when a scientific theory is held to have disproved a religious statement.

I have a great deal of sympathy for Karl Popper's confessed life-long dislike about theorising about God. "Theology, I still think, is due to lack of faith." However, I would want to add: "Science, I also think, is due to lack of knowledge." □

What the Inquisition taught the KGB

THE death penalty for heretics has a long history. As long ago as Plato it was believed, "if a person be guilty of impiety let him be punished with death." The early church viewed deviations from accepted belief with distaste and, perhaps mindful of the persecutions directed against Christians by the Roman Emperors before they embraced Christianity, were more tolerant. They anathematised and expelled the likes of Arius, who taught that Jesus was fully human.

A few hundred years of respectability and the attitude was hardening. Augustine was faced with militant Donatists, who were prepared to indulge in that shivery deviation—Second Baptism. At first he was afraid that persecution would produce nominal Christians, hypocrisy and fear clothing the lack of an orthodox foundation garment. But later in life Augustine declared: "He therefore who refuses to obey the imperial laws, when made against the truth of God acquires a great reward, he who refuses to obey when they are made for the support of the divine truth exposes himself to most grievous punishment."

By the time of the Middle Ages when the two swords of the secular and the spiritual were sheathed together in ruling Christendom, the official spokesman for orthodoxy, St Thomas Aquinas, could declare: "Heresy is a sin which merits not only excommunication but death, for it is worse to corrupt the faith which is the life of the soul than to issue counterfeit coins which administer to the secular life. Since counterfeiters were justly killed by Princes as enemies of the common good, so heretics deserve the same punishment." The police force for sniffing out these theological criminals was the notorious Inquisition.

Black cats

Most people imagine that the Inquisition terrorised the population, swooping like the Gestapo on wide-eyed villagers, dragging old women with black cats off to the nearest duckpond to be drowned as witches. This ignores the fear of revolution, militance or deviance which a static society like the Middle Ages fostered.

The zeal to conform and inform on their neighbours gave the Inquisition many willing helpers. The Cathars were a movement in Southern France who believed in a dual world of Spirit-Flesh, of Good and Evil fighting each other.

They became the baddies for a zealous section of the population. At Cambrai in 1076 a Cathar who had been judged heretical but not sentenced was being held in the local jail. He was seized by the mob and burned alive in a wooden box on the village green. The same thing happened in Strasbourg in 1114 when a mob feared clerical lenience towards a heretic and took matters into their own hands.

Of course there was only one religion, one church in those days. There was no salvation outside the church and no place within it for the deviant. The Reformation and the growth of different religious traditions within Western Europe enabled the dissident to apply for spiritual asylum in another denomination. Nonetheless there were spectacular trials such as those of Irving, McLeod Campbell and Robertson Smith within the Scottish Church last century.

In the present century Western Europe deals differently with its heretics of the spirit. A rebel Archbishop like Lefebre is put on suspension, a liberal theologian like Kung has his licence revoked.

We tend to believe that it is only in Iran that people who commit adultery are stoned, whereas in Europe it's the other way round. As for those countries who live under a non-religious dictatorship and are officially atheist, they appear to have learned a few things from the Inquisition. Stalin's

KGB managed to process more people through his concentration camps than the Inquisition managed through their courts. When the time came for Stalin to be removed from the atheist Pantheon as a heretic, it was done posthumously by transferring his corpse to an obscure place rather like a properly canonised saint having the procedure reversed. Today's Soviet dissidents are certified as insane and packed off to psychiatric wards.

Own sect

It's all so civilised, isn't it? Being a heretic today isn't dangerous at all. You have a wide choice of denominations—and if you feel particularly quarrelsome and contentious you can always set up your very own sect. It's no longer against the law. As for those with a more weird taste in religious deviation, they can join an exotic religion with saffron robes. Everything goes. *Chacon a son cult.*

The lesson of history is that doctrine becomes a cloak for power politics, rivalry becomes an excuse for dealing ruthlessly and the rule of fear, paranoia and suspicion means that whatsoever is not for us is against us. The innocent suffer and the conscientious are trodden down into conformity. This is what the new intolerance means. Let me be specific. If bringing the Kingdom means people in hospital beds being used in a power struggle between the parties, then something is far wrong. Strikes which damage the innocent are as justified in achieving the stated aim as burning heretics.

Of course we live in less barbarous times. The death certificates will not read—'victim of an industrial dispute' or 'death due to neglect of the National Health Service'. But they will just as surely have died because they were too weak in political muscle to be able to fight back. To have committed the heresy of being uncommitted to the right political dogma—or worse still being a political atheist may not mean the death penalty, but it sure is a heinous crime in the times we live in. □

Digging up a can of worms

REMEMBER the man who made a fortune out of a book which claimed that the Old Testament was really the story of how extra-terrestrials landed on earth or, to put it plainly, that Elijah's still small voice was a wee green man speaking in his ear? Do you also remember another New Testament scholar at Manchester who flipped and declared that the word 'Jesus' was really a code for a sacred mushroom and the Bible was a do-it-yourself manual for getting as high as the stars without leaving your body? Then a Professor of German Literature applied his literary mind to the Gospels and declared that they were a work of fiction and that Jesus had not actually existed?

For all lovers of trivial pursuits and other games, the names of the above

33

are respectively Erich Von Daniken, John Allegro and G. A. Wells. It does not take an intimate knowledge of logic, never mind Greek and Hebrew, to conclude that they cannot all be right. Indeed their respective influences upon the world of Biblical scholarship have been minimal. Nobody has bothered very much with their theories which have become imaginative curios to be put on the shelf with the books 'proving' that Queen Elizabeth I was a man, Queen Victoria had a love child, and that Pope John Paul I was murdered. For your information, if not for your conversion, let me bring you another in the line of startling books which turn upside down all that we ever believed about the Old Testament.

Debunking

The author of this latest debunking job is *Professor Kamal Salibi, of the American University in Beirut. While researching a book on the history of Arabia he was struck by the lack of early material, and while searching for place names of non-Arabic origin in a gazeteer recently produced in Riyadh, he found that nearly all the Biblical place names from the patriarchal period were concentrated in a small area of the Red Sea north of Yemen and far south of the traditional sites in Palestine. He deduced that the nomadic Hebrews had their origins there and had brought no more than a handful of the place names with them when they eventually settled in Palestine.

* The Bible Came From Arabia, by Kamal Salibi (Cape, £10.95).

He argues that while only a few of the Palestinian sites have been linked by archaeology with the Bible, the bulk of the names in the Yemen area are to be found stated in the Bible and that this was where Abraham, the Caravan King, had his home and it was here that the Israelites settled after they had crossed the Red Sea with Moses.

Right away you may ask why no one has noticed this before. Professor Salibi reasons this is because Nebuchanezzar in 586BC put an end to this Jewish enclave in lands that eventually were to become the heartland of Mohammed the Prophet. The other reason was that the relationship remained disguised because the Jewish scriptures underwent a change/distortion at the hands of the Massoretic scribes.

Distortions

Originally the Jewish Bible was written in Classical Hebrew with no vowels. Most verbs had three consonants, and it was these scribes who superimposed a system of vowels which became the standard text. Salibi says that the Massoretes had lost touch with the language of the Bible and made many distortions. For example, it was no wonder that scholars have searched in vain for Mount Horeb on Sinai since it should be Harib—and this is to be found in the Yemen area. Usually sentences without vowels can be deduced easily. 'CT ST N T MT,' will soon be exposed by crossword buffs as 'The cat sat on the mat,' but place names are not so easily guessed by context.

Thus H-YRDN (which is translated throughout the Bible as Jordan) is not the name of a river but means the 'Ridge' and refers to a huge escarpment which dominates Asir and explains, says Salibi, why the Old Testament nowhere makes reference to the Jordan as a river. King David's Zion, he maintains, is a mere 80km away (Siyan) from Jerusalem (the village of Al-Sharim) where, sad to say, archaeological digging is banned. This last fact means that many aspects of Salibi's theory cannot as yet be put to the test. The proof will be in the digging.

Flying a kite

The implications of the book's theory is that Israeli claims to statehood in Palestine are founded upon a false assumption and that the Jewish homeland lies just down the road from Mecca. It is not just a can of worms that the professor has been adigging. He is flying a kite—and good luck to him, but I am sure like me you will not be surprised to find that his kite blows away and is covered by the sands of time.

I have often suspected that by raking through the telephone directory according to a number code, you could extract a secret message. Graffiti such as 'Kilroy was here' may be interpreted by future scholars to mean that Bonnie Prince Charlie stopped there. (The French-born King or ROI-GEDDIT??) It just takes an ingenious mind and an ability to do crosswords and you can prove anything with words. So until I hear otherwise I am going to go on think-

ing of Jerusalem as a place where Arab, Jew and Christian have a crossroads and a task to effect reconciliation that will take deeds, not words, to achieve.

All the magic of scholars cannot turn this sacred toadstool into a real living Holy City. That needs prophets who are usually stoned, which unless you choose to think that means they are high on drugs in an ecstatic vision, means, they suffer before the words become reality. □

Examining the Bible down to the last letter

IN the beginning was J, D, E, and P. These were the genesis of Genesis. They gave themselves away by their distinctive styles. They had their own pet name for God—He was Jehovah to one, the Lord of Hosts to another who used a plural form. But there is unity in diversity and just as the Hebrews developed their monotheistic religion out of the mish-mash of cults in Palestine, so the unity of the Book of Genesis developed out of sacred writings.

There are no by-lines in the Bible, so it was left to scholars a century ago to identify the hidden signatures behind the Pentateuch, the Five Books of the Law, which is the core of the Old Testament. Its five books retell and overlap the ancient stories of how God created Man and after generations of wandering around living a life which makes Wild West movies look tame, there was captivity in Egypt and then liberation to the Promised Land. They were strong stuff these Tales of the Wild East, which included gang rapes, homosexual orgies, incest, fratricide. There were love stories—among them the lovely tale of how Rebekah's father tricked Jacob into doing double time for his daughter. There is adventure and above all there is a moral. A very strong dose of moral medicine indeed. Two tablets of stone to be taken once in every lifetime.

According to legend the Pentateuch was written by Moses just as the Psalms were written by David. Digging through the literary evidence the biblical detectives found not one set of fingerprints but at least four. So they begat J, D, E, and P.

Computer

Now an atheist computer has declared its lack of belief in these gentlemen and, to howls of delight from fundamentalists in both Jewish and Christian religions, has made it possible that Ol' Grampa Moses was the culprit after all. The computer was programmed by Jewish scholars to examine the text for differences of word usage in much the same way that Shakespeare's plays or Paul's letters have been examined to determine whether they were written by their putative authors. Who would have thought that the tablets on which the Ten Commandments were written could be encapsulated in a microchip?

A great deal depends on what the computer was programmed to ask and the criteria for writing the programme might not prove acceptable to all Old Testament scholars. The theory of multiple authorship is more usual in explaining repetitions such as the Creation story appearing in two different (and slightly contradictory) accounts. Of course, Moses might have been going senile and got a bit mixed up.

The issue may not seem very important, unless you happen to believe that the authority of a book rests entirely on its authorship. But even if you are convinced that David wrote the Psalms and Moses write the Pentateuch there are still a lot of other books in the Old Testament.

Indeed its Hebrew title takes account of this diversity—'Law, Prophets and Writings.' The writings range from wisdom literature, such as Proverbs and Ecclesiastes, to fictional tales with a message, such as Ruth and Jonah. They include poetry of the Renaissance period known as the Solomonic Enlightenment.

Reliable

Among the prophets there are even surprises. Isaiah was not one person but three. But if schizophrenia made Van Gogh a better painter so the spectrum of writing in the Bible makes it a more reliable testament of the religious life of man.

When the New Testament is put under the detective's magnifying glass, several whodunnits emerge. The biggest is the Synoptic Problem. It consists of the Eternal Triangle of

Matthew, Mark and Luke and which one copied from the others. Most scholars would agree that Mark came first and the other two used him in writing their accounts. There are other clues that Matthew had an accomplice called 'Q'.

As far as I know computers have not yet been brought to bear on the Synoptic Problem which has been tossed around for a century. It is interesting because it gives a tiny glimpse into the mind and intention of the Gospel writers. Why did they choose to omit a particular miracle and why did they change the chronology elsewhere?

The Fourth Gospel, that of John, places the cleansing of the Temple near the beginning, whereas the Synoptics have it near the climax of Jesus' confrontation with the authorities. John presumably saw it as a figurative event which symbolised the purpose of Jesus' ministry. He was writing much later than the others.

John uses a term which the others do not. He speaks of the *Logos* made flesh. The Logos is usually translated as the Word, but it has a stronger meaning. It is guiding principle, abiding truth. So it means the Truth incarnate as well as the Word incarnate. So the original word was made flesh, turned into words and the computer can turn the words into guesses at the Origin of the Word.

Even if it should emerge that Moses survived longer than Methuselah and stayed alive in a monastery on top of Mount Sinai writing all the other later books of the Bible, including the Gospels, I would not be upset. The important thing about the Bible is that its words be translated into actions. When that happens it becomes more amazing than any word processor made of microchips. □

BODY

Gut reactions and indigestible facts...

Why the Orange Walk should be banned

JULY is the season of the year when the sound of the flute is heard in the land and a section of the population migrate up and down the streets going cuckoo. Yes its Orange Walk season, when we are invited to rejoice in celebrating the victory of King William of Orange (or Good King Billy as he is known in some circles) at the Battle of the Boyne.

The fact that he did so with the help of Catholic mercenaries and received a letter of congratulations from the Pope has been overtaken by the mythology that this was a victory for Protestantism.

My knowledge of this period of history is rather hazy so I am not going to make an issue of it either way, for the simple reason which I suspect is shared by many of you, that I don't care. The result of the battle seems rather far removed from the issues facing the world today. But while on the subject of confessing ignorance, I must also state that I have so far made it through life without witnessing or participating in an Orange Walk. That is, until this year.

No, I have not been secretly induct-ed as a Grand Master of Tangerine Terror. It is simply that I was brought up in the East of Scotland and have lived in places whither the Orange-men walketh not, neither in triumph nor provocation. This may seem strange to those who would think that Religious Affairs Correspondents would have the Glorious Twelfth of July firmly written in their diaries.

Since I have never regarded the matter as having much bearing on religious affairs then this omission on my part is logical, if somewhat lacking in curiosity. Recently my curiosity was satisfied when I attempted to drive into the centre of Glasgow from the West End. The great cavalcade was on the move. The traffic was not. So I abandoned my car and watched from a pedestrian walkway high above Charing Cross.

It was loud. It was colourful, even tuneful. And it was never ending. Band after band, some consisting of pretty wee girls dressed like drum majorettes, but unfortunately not exhibiting the skills of those alluring maidens from across the Atlantic, the baton-twirlers. In front of each band walked a Big Man with a big stick. Some of these bowler-hatted chaps looked like bouncers from the Palais de dance, the protuberance of the ample stomachs bouncing forward with each beat of the drum.

They bore an uncanny resemblance to Robbie Coltrane's television caricature Orangeman.

So why does this free entertainment not qualify for the description of good clean fun? First because the behaviour of many of the marchers is in the worst traditions of bigotry, drunkenness and loutishness. It is worse when it uses the Walk as an occasion for provocation, as in Northern Ireland where detours through Catholic areas have been planned. Riots ensued when the police diverted the marchers, prompting the then Northern Ireland Secretary, Mr Douglas Hurd, to describe some Orangemen as a disgrace to the name of Loyalists.

Most of us would agree with any condemnation of such conduct. But what about peaceful Orange Walks, if experience will allow you to admit such a possibility? Well, I would ban them too if I had my way. My reason is that our cities are now designed round the motor car. Allowing thousands of marchers through city streets in the middle of the day is to throw a spanner into the works of a large and complex machine. It is an act of public disorder in itself.

Never mind the opinions or the colour or the creed of the marchers, they have no God-given right to disrupt the life of a city. We do not allow motor cyclists on to the roads without helmets, so why should we allow bowler-hatted men with batons to walk up the highways?

No doubt some will defend the right to march on grounds of civil liberties for they will swiftly perceive that if I were to get my way, all kinds of trade union demonstrations to say nothing of peace marches would fall under the ban.

To which I would answer—why not? Society has changed since the days of the cart and horse, or since men with red flags walked in front of cars at the same speed as the Orange Walk. Why should a thousand people be given licence by the district council to do what an individual would be arrested for doing, and why should the police who would arrest you or I for doing it, be paid overtime out of the public purse to stand and watch this organised chaos wend its way across the city?

This is not civil liberty but plain silliness. It is not as if alternatives do not exist. They are called public parks. Here the marchers can drill up and down to their hearts' content. Why not the Orange Walk at Bellahouston Park? It is big enough for the bands to circle without getting in each other's way or drowning each other out.

The Orangemen could even talk to those trees (the ones removed and replanted for the Papal visit in 1982 about which the parks department is still very sensitive and reluctant to comment) on the basis that plants respond to music.

They might even find that the trees prefer flute bands to papal choirs. Who knows? But a battle of the bands is preferable any day to the Battle of the Boyne or what has increasingly become a battle on the streets. □

Side to homosexuality that isn't so gay

GAY—a tiny trinity of letters which used to mean joyous, happy and fun-loving. Now it has another meaning. It is the self-designation preferred by those who used to be known as queers, poofs, homos, by those who like to call a spade a bloody shovel. Less direct forms of allusion are practised in different sections of society. Bent (as a nine-bob note); camp (as a row of tents). There seems to be rather a lot of names for those who share a proclivity for their own sex.

Of course there is a lot of it about. There always has been. The Greeks discovered electricity and quite a lot of them were AC-DC as well. The Romans had baths together and young men to towel them dry. And let us not forget the men of Sodom, the original buggers (in the proper sense of that much used word).

In case you do not read the dirty parts of the Bible, then let me remind you that the city of Sodom was earmarked for divine retribution when Abraham pleaded for it to be spared. God sent two angels to check out the city and the men of Sodom tried to kidnap them from their host, Lot, in order to have homosexual relations with them.

The original Hebrew does not quite spell that out in detail, but that was what was meant, and has forever attached itself to the sin of sodomy which was until recently against the law and still is with those under 21 years of age.

However, what has changed a great deal is the public attitude to homosexuality. There was always a place for the camp characters who asked: "Are you being served?" and ordered "Shut that door", but about them there was always ambiguity. Those who 'came out' and directly declared their homosexuality were regarded as brave and courageous. They were automatically members of a minority which was loathed and persecuted by a substantial section of society. Jeers were the least of it. Beatings by boot boys were probably the worst of it.

In most professions it was suicide to admit to being a homosexual, and in some macho jobs like bricklaying it was probably asking for a brick to be dropped upon one's head. Sniggers and the double meanings surrounded the subject which was one of the biggest taboos in our society.

In an age when totems and taboos are reduced to being another manifestation of Freudian symbols, where stands the homosexual? Rampant. That's where he stands. He has moved from being a persecuted minority to a person with full and equal 'rights'.

Now you may argue that he always had equal right provided he did not indulge in anal intercourse and I would agree with you. But that is not enough for the Gay Liberationists. They want to assert that homosexual relationships are just as valid as heterosexual ones and that it is perfectly 'natural' for some people to be homosexual if their inclination is in that direction and that those who profess distaste for homosexuality are denying them human rights.

Oh dear, it's always human rights is it not? When emotions get steamed up, it's human rights that become the issue.

It is not dislike of homosexuals which has prompted me to tackle this subject. It is the abuse of freedom which homosexuals have won which distresses me. I do not think that people should be in jail for doing things with one another in a closet. Like many I would draw the line if it were a water closet frequented by the public, but prison is not a place for such offenders. Nor do I think that it is disgraceful if two men of a loving disposition should set up home together. Such a relationship has produced some of the finest English music this century and it is no secret that Tchaikovsky was homosexual as were many of the great creative minds through the ages.

No one should be forced into conformity which conflicts with their true nature.

But—and it is a big but—being of a homosexual disposition is a very different matter from indulging in sodomy. Yet the Gay Lobby will not allow a line to be drawn by those of us who do not feel threatened by homosexuals but who would argue that sodomy is both unnatural, unhealthy and immoral at the very least.

Let me take these in turn. Unnatural is easy. We could not reproduce our human race if it were. Unhealthy it most certainly is (I have been prevailed upon to refrain from detailing how) but one only has to say the magic word AIDS to realise the sad fact that the consequences of some homosexual intercourse are far from gay.

The argument on moral grounds is not so easy. Who is to say what manner of intimacy is right and what is wrong? Gay Rights spokesmen would presumably lay claim to a right to enjoy a full physical relationship which is just as valid as that which is enjoyed by heterosexuals. They would argue that what is moral for heterosexuals is moral for homosexuals. That immediately poses a difficulty. Heterosexuals can marry but there is no such recognised category as "gay marriage" (except perhaps in Denmark), so right away we have to tear up the book of rules.

But rather than be diverted by the red herring of whether or not such a category should exist or by the tricky question of how love should be expressed outwith marriage, let us not look for the borderline. Let us instead look at the point which is well beyond it, indeed completely over the score.

I am referring to a level of promiscuity which even the most liberal heterosexual would regard as immoral. Let us say for the sake of argument that it is five different partners on the same night. Now if I were to suggest to you that in some gay bars the 'lads' pop off to the toilets that number of times to indulge themselves, then you might think I was repeating lurid propaganda put about by the puritan league. Not so. The figure was mentioned to me by the manager of a gay bar who was justifying the role of the establishment, but added, "some of them are not angels you know. They come in here for one orange juice and they're up and down to the loos five times in one night with different blokes." If that is not over the score I do not know what is.

I am resisting the temptation to thunder about AIDS being a judgment upon them, etc. Brutality and callousness are never justified, even in response to disgusting conduct. Many homosexuals are gentle and loving people who have neither physical nor promiscuous relationships. There is also apparently no link between homosexuality and child abuse, although most normal boys pass through a homosexual fantasy period in adolescence. (Please note I have said nothing about female homosexuality since some of the above arguments do not apply, so will lesbians please save themselves a stamp).

There is much hypocrisy practised against homosexuals and I hope not to contribute to it, but it is not all on the one side. For some gays it is 'gay right or wrong,' a licence to do as they will which must surely be condemned. It is not yet an issue of epidemic proportions with the gays of the world about to suffer the fate of the citizens of Sodom. But surely the rest of us can ask that some responsible members of the self-styled Gay community will condemn such excesses. Instead they seem to close ranks against any criticism and label it persecution.

Labels and name-calling are not life and death matters. AIDS is, and if the gays do not respect self control, then the rest of us will be entitled to ask whether, having acquired human rights, they are unwilling to extend them to others. □

Blue jokes and the sayings of Smith

A WISECRACKING RABBI who was sacked by his congregation for his saucy remarks failed in his attempt to be reinstated to his Southgate Synagogue. The joker, 36-year-old Clifford Cohen, failed to persuade a London industrial tribunal that his conduct and remarks (such as "one drink and she's anybody's" when a little girl tripped during a barmitzvah) were becoming. Thus he has gone.

Such a transitory career as a rabbi suggests to me a new saying—'sick humourists transit ingloriously'. Those who live dangerously end up without a living. Thankfully this fate has not befallen a splendid exponent of rabbinical humour, Rabbi Lionel Blue. A regular contributor to Radio Four's Thought for the Day, this witty gentleman can even outquip the presenters, and you have to get up early in the morning to do that.

His patter is now issued on a cassette in which he tells the story of how he was baptised as Christian. He had gone to stay at a monastery and somehow a misunderstanding arose and he was asked if he had been baptised. No, he replied, and before he knew it his hosts, oblivious of his religious upbringing, had offered this sacrament to him. Too polite to refuse their generosity, he went through the ceremony.

The po-faced and the pious may not find that funny, but to hear him tell it and keep a straight face is a considerable feat.

Wits among the clergy are much in demand, not only on Thought for the Day. Wedding receptions and Burns Suppers would not be the same without them. The Kirk's answer to the rollicking rabbis was of course Revd

James Currie. Armed with his Bumper Fun Book, the minister of Dunlop joked his way around the world at various functions. St Andrew's Night in Nigeria; Burns Suppers in America; Fiddlers' Rallies in Dunoon; Ceilidhs in the Holy Land.

The late James Currie had in common with all comedians a voracious appetite for new material. Hence the Bumper Fun Book into which new jokes and stories were put. Indeed the Reverend gentleman could often be seen scribbling frantically during other toasts putting new gems into the book.

Once he was doing this during a speech by Jimmy Logan who caught sight of the scribbling out of the corner of his eye. "Am I going too fast for you, Jimmy?" he quipped. As he began another story he paused and turned to Jimmy Currie with a twinkle in his eye: "Don't bother taking this one down Jimmy—I got it from you."

But the greatest and most original clergy wit of all time must surely be Revd Sydney Smith (1771–1845). The Hogarth Press republished Hesketh Pearson's 1934 biography *The Smith of Smiths*. Whether dining in the glittering salons of Mayfair or ministering to the sick in Yorkshire or Somerset, Smith reduced all who met him to a state of breathless mirth.

His wit not only aimed to amuse but also to reform. Through the pages of the Edinburgh Review of which he was a founding figure, from the pulpit, in lectures and pamphlets, Smith challenged political, social, and religious cant. The poor, American slaves, Irish Catholics or the hypocrisy of war were all causes dear to his Whiggish heart and he scandalised the Establishment of his day. He was not just ahead of his times, but a timeless figure whose prophetic words were cast as perceptive wit.

It was the overly loquacious Lord Macaulay who called him the Smith of Smiths. When Macaulay lay in bed ill once, Sydney paid a pastoral call and pronounced: "He is more agreeable than I have ever seen him. There were some gorgeous flashes of silence."

It was Smith who said of someone, "He imagines heaven as pate de foie gras to the sound of trumpets." He liked the good things of life but he was no sybarite. As a pastor he was diligent and although iconoclastic, he defended the clergy against outside attack. A squire once angrily said to him: "If I had a son who was an idiot by Jove I'd make him a parson". Without batting an eyelid Sydney retorted: "But I see your father was of a different mind."

Here are just a few examples of his *bon mots*: .

"Benevolence is a natural instinct of the human mind. When A sees B in grievous distress, his conscience always urges him to entreat C to help him."

"There is not the least use in preaching to anyone unless you chance to catch them ill."

"I must believe in the Apostolic Succession, there being no other way of accounting for the descent of the Bishop of Exeter from Judas Iscariot."

High Church snobbery and cultism were anathema to him but his ripostes were as always stylish. When a Puseyite wrote to him, dating his letter by a Saint's Day, Sydney replied by heading his page 'Washing Day'. He said of holy relics: "England is almost the only country in the world where there is not some favourite religious spot where absurd lies, little bits of cloth, feathers, splinters, rusty nails and other invaluable relics are treasured up and in defence of which the whole population are willing to turn out and perish as one man."

Despite this distaste for the excesses of Catholic piety his record on toleration and the emancipation of Catholics was good. It is tempting in today's church situation to say of Smith what his contemporary Wordsworth said of Milton. "O Sydney wouldst thou were living at this hour!" □

Manners that have gone by the board

IT is, I am reliably informed by one whose manners are of the best, perfectly correct when served dinner to begin to eat even if table companions have not yet been served. This information has, I understand, the authority of Debrett's behind it. It is quite a different matter to begin to eat before one's companions at a table over which Grace is about to be pronounced.

As a hungry little lad my stomach occasionally overruled my manners

and the Grace would include a parenthetic rebuke such as, "For what we are about to receive (and for what Stewart has already eaten) we give You thanks . . ."

It was all gently done. A tongue in cheek reminder to someone whose cheeks were bulging with bad manners. Of course you might want to take a very purist line and say that it is bad manners to remind others of their bad manners. Thus when you are the only person to get up when a lady comes into the room, or when everyone has half finished their food and you are still waiting for Grace, by standing up, for failing to lift fork and knife, you are drawing attention to the sins of omission of the others and silently rebuking them. Is that goody goody or is it just good manners? Oh dear, it's all so confusing.

One source of authority on such matters was also royalty. The royal family could be relied upon as paragons of etiquette. Many is the time I have been able at my grandmother's table to lick my fingers after eating a cream coronet upon a precedent established by good Queen Mary who had been observed doing such a thing by no less than my grandmother when visiting the big house.

I dined out on that one for quite a while, but have not had occasion to be offered cream coronets of late. The last time I was offered them was at a Free Kirk soiree and I was careful to keep my fingers to myself until after the Grace.

Saying Grace is not always a prelude to conventional manners in Free Kirk households as I once found when asked to offer the Grace in a cottage in Point, Lewis, in which the great aunt of a friend lived. The old lady, clad in a woolly mutch, sat head bowed, with her cup of tea in her hand.

When I had finished and opened my eyes I noted that she had the cup in one hand and the saucer in the other. Alas, I mused, the poor old soul has slobbed her tea. Not so. Great Aunt S was simply pouring her tea into the saucer, whereupon she drank it down with a loud slurp.

Later I gathered she did not think much of my manners. I was not a proper minister since I had no dog collar on and my Grace had been far too short. The venerable are not therefore always the definitive word on matters of etiquette, but there was always royalty. Or so I thought, until I read this week that Prince Charles, who was held up to my by that self-same grandmother as a paragon, has apparently gone the way of the rest of our post-war generation.

The publishing director of *Burke's Peerage* is apparently concerned that the Prince (and even more so the Princess) of Wales are letting the side down in matters of etiquette. They behave as equals. She precedes him rather than staying behind as befits a consort. They kiss in public. They go to "vulgar nouveau riche" places like Palm Beach on a royal visit.

"No doubt," said Mr Harold Brooks-Baker of Burke's, "it fits in with the freer ways of today but some feel that freedom is an over-used word. One only hopes that these new waters they are navigating lead to a safe haven." I suppose that is as outspoken as an expert on etiquette can dare become in digging the dirt with his agricultural implement instead of a spade.

In answering this criticism Prince Charles would have been of impeccable good manners in employing the seven degrees of retort by Touchstone outlined in Shakespeare's *As You Like It*. "As you have books for good manners I will name you the degrees. The first, the Retort Courteous; the second, the Quip Modest; the third, the Reply Churlish; the fourth, the Reproof Valiant; the fifth, the Countercheck Quarrelsome; the sixth, the Lie with Circumstance; the seventh, the Lie Direct." The moral of this passage is that in rejecting criticism you work up from gentle fun-poking and comment, through rebuke before calling your critic a damned liar.

"Evil communications corrupt good manners," says a Greek proverb, and in the polarised world we live in, where name calling and counter-check is the order of the day, it is not surprising that good manners and etiquette have gone by the board.

In this post-welfare state, travellers are reminded of their duty to give up their seat to old ladies by a designated seat, post offices cannot trust the customers to queue so they erect mazes through which one must wind before being served. Where there are no manners, order must be enforced.

Meanwhile small niceties, like covering one's mouth when yawning or refraining from whistling loudly in public places, remain sadly neglected by legislators. Of course five yawns would justify one in administering the Countercheck Quarrelsome—perhaps by saying how much you admire the person's handsome tonsils.

But when all the please and thank you is unsaid and the little courtesy is undone, it does make a difference to society. Etiquette and good manners are not a middle-class pastime or an optional extra for nice people.

Slamming a door in someone's face has nothing to do with breeding or upbringing. It displays a basic lack of respect for other human beings. In other words, manners not only make the man, but lack of them make men into animals.   □

Architects and gravestones of a generation

EXCEPT the architect build the house they labour in vain that build it. You'll pardon the paraphrase I hope. It should probably read, "except the architect supervise the building of the house, etc." This is of course what architects are supposed to do. But faults in execution of buildings are often blamed on poor workmanship by the builder. Never, never the perfect design by the architect. So here we go, boot toecaps are suitably polished, draw the leg back slowly and stand by to put a large boot into architects. Well, some architects. Or even some architects occasionally. Or perhaps some architects some of the time. You see you never can tell where the fault lies. The chaps were only trying their best.

I mean, how would you like to live in one of these funny houses with black bricks down one wall and double glazing covering the others? These architect chaps don't have it easy. We expect so much of them. They design wonderful housing schemes for us to live in. High rise. Lovely view. They don't know that someone will vandalise the elevators and pee on the stairs. We can't blame them that vandals spray paint on the walls. All right—so there are no pubs and shops. Since when was it the right of council house tenants to have facilities along with their accommodation?

Admittedly things are not what they were in the 'sixties when architects could rely on plenty of money from generous Governments to build lots of colleges. The architects were a lot smarter than the Governments. They knew that the boom in students wouldn't last. They knew that cut backs in education would force closures.

So what did they do? They made the colleges really monstrous. Concrete and glass lavatories on a grand scale. Easily flushed away. They knew that if you made schools and universities permanent structures, tooled beautifully in stone and designed in a timeless way to permit the flowering of reflective thought and ancient customs, that society would become attached to them and wouldn't want to let them go when the cutbacks came. So they followed their cousins in the car industry and made their buildings with built-in obsolescence.

Of course the ideal illustration of the foolish devotion of the populace to semi-permanent structures is in religion. The architect knows only too well how devoted they become to a building once it is erected. Look at the way Kirk folk fighting a union of congregations revere the work of the Victorian architects (even the different examples) to see how true that is. The modern architect makes sure his church and his school are built of less stern stuff, for the landscape around them is of shifting sand. So why make the foundations permanent?

Of course architects are human and it must be seen that such an approach is liable to make the architect a pariah figure, unbeloved of the society in which his creations are set. Not for British architects the spoiled role of their Finnish counterparts who command the same prestige in society as pop stars do in Western society.

Prestige and a little bit of reward are not easy to come by. So should we be surprised that the architect has to content himself with high fees most of the time as his reward when an ungrateful society refuses to thank him? There are other ways of course. There are prizes which can be awarded within the architecture profession.

Little wonder the architects invented their prizes. If the Fuhrer asks you to build only concentration camps, where can you win any campaign medals except by inventing them?

Little wonder then that the Iona Community in launching its competition to design a MacLeod Centre on Iona to accommodate pilgrims was inundated with entries. Architects are said to have been prowling on the island incognito gathering intelligence for their mission. There could have even been a Spot the Architect competition to go along with the design competition.

These poor chaps were searching desperately for a project which would not be cursed with the ephemeral vulgarity of their usual tasks. They can hardly design a Mulberry harbour and tented village for Iona which has held out against the ravages of the Atlantic, the Viking, the climate, and the disinterest of the Scot in his religious heritage.

Good luck to them, then. They have a high mark to shoot at and a long tradition to maintain. If their vanity in pursuit of the prize should carry them away, they will be suitably chastised in the words of Psalm 124: 'Except the Lord shall build the house, they labour in vain that build it.'

That text is not aimed at architects or socialist town councils, but at all of us. It challenges us to express our dreams in buildings which will stand the test of time, for they are the gravestones of our generation. □

Service with stupidity, not a smile

THEY are everywhere. Harridan women employed in the so-called service industries. What a bad joke and misnomer that is. People who are supposed to give service but instead give cheek, insolence, surliness, non co-operation, stupidity and render sourness, not service.

Of course, it does not always hit you between the eyes with such immediate aggression. Stupid they may be but not lacking in guile. They make the rule book mentality into an art form and could easily get a PhD in bureaucracy. They also make mistakes, but part of the game is that they never apologise. Occasionally they concede or compromise. But they never apologise.

What, you may ask, has brought on this fit of choler on my part? Why have I decided to attack the fair sex (that's another joke when applied to some of the gross matrons and thin-lipped minxes I have in mind). Part of the answer is that the vast majority of service personnel who answer telephones, serve in shops and deal with the great British public are female. Thus it is not their sex but their preponderance that moves me on the grounds of statistical fairness to refer to them as she.

If you are moving house and making purchases, dealing with public utilities (gas, electricity, telephones) then she will confront you. She will make it clear right from the start by her tone of voice that it is with tired reluctance that she has decided to deal with you at all. Turning up the charm level at this point is as effective as spraying DDT in her eye. She will not respond except to indicate that you are a chancer or a smoothie who is attempting to circumvent the proper rules and procedures.

Rules and procedures. These are the gospel by which she lives. The mere suggestion that these might not apply to the specific situation in which you find yourself, is to incur the curling lip (or snide tone if over the telephone) and the trenchant reiteration of the particular rule. (For instance: "We can't deal with that until department X has authorised us.") "But," you protest, "I'm telling you now." This leads to the third repetition of the rule with the implied tone that you are stupid or deaf.

It is at this point that I slip from my pedestal of polite insouciance. "That's not very imaginative," I rejoin. "Well that's the procedure," she says with threatening finality, because this is your final warning to submit to her domination. Needless to say I fail to heed this warning.

"It's a silly procedure then," I find myself saying, and the confrontation has become war. She has dealt with my like before. Indeed every second customer is probably just like me, but the charade is going to be played out on the basis that I am being difficult. That way she can keep her puritanical role as keeper of the rules, and I can be represented as a rude anarchist. I fall for the trap. "Why can't you do so-and-so?" I rasp with the confidence of someone who is offering a constructive alternative, but with the sharp edge of a man who is losing patience.

It is of course an absudity that I am suggesting. It is not covered by the rules which she has been taught. It is by definition absurd, but it is also threatening to the stolid supremacy she exercises. I have become enemy. She deploys her heavy artillery. "I'll get the supervisor," she spits, and is gone before you have a chance to say, "don't bother." But since you have come this far you wait (usually for some time) until the supervisor emerges. She is simply an older version of the woman you have just been talking to, and so the farce goes into Round Two with defeat for the customer the only possible outcome.

The archetype of these harridans is the Glasgow clippie of c'mon gerraff fame. Their daughters and their children's children hath spread throughout the land of Greater Glasgow. While it is true that the warmth of hospitality, generosity and friendliness to be found in the West of Scotland has no equal, it is also true that the depths of rudeness and disgustingly mannered carelessness that passes for ethnic character are rarely surpassed.

Lest it be thought that the matriachs are supreme in this artless craft of rendering service into an offensive act, it has to be said that the Glasgow cabbie is in a class of his own.

I once asked a taxi driver to take me to the Glasgow Herald offices whither I was to hand in my weekly scribblings. It was not a paper he ever read, he informed me. He preferred the Daily Record which was much better than the Glasgow Herald. I ignored the contradiction upon which his judgment was based since if he did not read a paper he could not assess its worth. Eventually I interrupted the diatribe to point out that I was paying him to take me to the newspaper, not for his opinions about it. This did not go down well and I was nearly ejected from the cab.

Sadly, it appears to be generally accepted that this is the way people in service industries in Glasgow behave. Am I wrong to refuse to capitulate to this tawdry behaviour? Am I naive or snobbish in thinking that better standards ought to be enforced by the employers? It is easy to pretend that the values and standard of behaviour about which I am speaking are genteel or middle class. Piffle.

Since when was it middle class or bourgeois to take a pride in your work, to want to see customers whose patronage provides your salary, satisfied? Is it too much to ask that the boorish Directory Enquiry operator tries again to find a telephone number you know exits? The young MFI salesman who is only concerned in making sure the commission on your purchase accrues to him, not his colleague, has forgotten why he is there in the first place.

This is not a political or class matter. Nor a question of manners, or a moral issue concerned with how those who serve the public behave. It is a stewardship question. It asks how service personnel use their position to help the customer; how the eight hours of their day are spent. If it is in awarding themselves points for putdowns of the public then they should give up their jobs, live on welfare, and be rude to their friends. There are surely plenty of unemployed people who for long were treated as less than human, who now long for the chance to demonstrate their humanity in helping others, and doing it with a smile. □

Striking a blow against brutality of boxing

THERE was a time when nice respectable people were not revolted by the sport of bear baiting. They probably didn't attend, but they didn't do anything to stop it. Ditto cock fighting. Indeed the habits of our civilised forebears at work and play would not always stand up to the scrutiny of the modern conscience.

Little boys scrambled up chimneys in Victorian times. Who else would be able to get the job done? Pit ponies trotted up and down mineshafts. Had not God made them small enough to do the job? And they didn't leave the fumes behind them that an engine might have done.

There must have been a time when each of these practices ceased to be tolerable and reasonable behaviour. I'm not suggesting that legislators woke up one morning and said: "We must abolish slavery!" or "Bear baiting must cease!", but for the position to have changed from tacit acceptance to wholesale condemnation, there must have been a fulcrum point when the arguments tipped decidedly in one direction.

One cannot help wondering what practices condoned by our contemporary society will fall foul of tomorrow's humane conscience. Bull fighting suggests itself as one immediately, but it is hardly rampant in Britain. Cigarette smoking may prove yet to be as anachonistic to twenty-first century citizens as snuff-taking is to our own age. But I have an inkling which sport may be missing from the Olympiad of the future.

No, I don't mean marathon running, although I am certain that the spectators of the original run from the Battle of Marathon to Athens would be astonished to learn that we regard such things as sports, since the man who ran the original dropped dead on arrival. Much as I regard them as a social nuisance on a par with the Orange Walk and invented by the devil to prevent churchgoers getting to church on time, I cannot claim that marathons have (yet) been proved to kill enough people to justify banning them.

My nominee for the non-sport of the future is one which I used to watch on television regularly. Its heroes are household names and millions of pounds are at stake when it is staged. It is played between two people in a small arena and the object is to hit the opponent on the head so that his cerebrum thwacks against his skull with sufficient force to cause loss of consciousness. Yes, folks, I mean boxing.

Please do not tell me that the object of professional boxing is to accumulate points by touching parts of the opponent's head. I would be exceedingly naive if I believed that. The object is to win—and the way to

53

achieve this is to knock out the opponent. But just consider what this means rendering him unconscious. It means inflicting an injury which would be severely punished by a court of law if it was inflicted during an argument. Witnesses would be called who would give testimony about the effects of such concussion upon the brain physiology. Still more damning evidence could be brought about the long-term effect of punches to the head.

Boxing at the very least means inflicting cuts and bruises on another human being. No amount of dressing it up in fancy language or elegant commentating will alter that. To my mind it is as much of a prostitution of literary talent as Hemingway committed by his glorification of bullfighting, to read the likes of Allan Massie, lending his elegant prose to the description of pugilists, praising boxing as an art-form as if they were opera singers engaged in an aria celebrating physical courage in a coloratura of fists.

Nor do I regard the villains of the piece as the fighters themselves. They are the victims. Very few of them seem to have profited from their careers in anything but a short-term way. Even the Greatest himself, Cassius Clay, alias Muhammed Ali, who seemed to have had a highly successful career during which a minimal number of punches were landed to his head, has suffered a brain condition which it is difficult to believe is unconnected with his trade.

It is the aptly-named 'promoters' who are the ones to blame in the history of boxing. It is they who plucked starving kids from the back streets and made them into heroes before they sank into oblivion mentally and metaphorically. Benny Lynch is an example close enough to home.

But it should perhaps be said that amateur boxers often avoid the excesses and the injuries of their professional colleagues, and the likes of Dick MacTaggart is a monument to sportsmanlike behaviour. But how typical is he of the sport? The boxer hero is more likely to be a nasty thug who glares at his opponent at the weigh-in and acts like Mr Nasty. In terms of image the heavyweights are the heavyweights.

As for the fans, I can summon up little sympathy for dinner-jacketed men who sit around tables with their belts bulging while boxers spatter their tuxedo with blood as a cabaret act. As for the moral angle, I can hardly see that even muscular Christianity can underwrite such a sport. I suppose you could argue that we should turn the other cheek, but that seems like tempting fate when dealing with a boxer.

My guess is that I am not alone in waking up to the stunning brutality of boxing. True, it is often a manifestation of courage and masculine strength. But to see how false this justification, let us play the equality card. Let us imagine boxing without the masculinity. Let us imagine two ladies slugging hell out of one another in a ring. Where is the courage in that? □

Punishment and role of religion

BIRCH them, hang them, or flog them. This is the big stick treatment for violent criminals which is traditionally associated with an extreme Right-wing attitude. We have moved away from such remedies as being too brutal for a humane society and nowadays those who advocate them are seen as blimpish relics of an imperialist, authoritarian society which favoured cold baths and weals on the buttocks as character forming.

Retribution is now a dirty word. Punishment is something which is very rarely associated with virtue, and more often is undertaken with reluctance. Punitive measures become sanctions which will encourage offenders not to do it again, rather than righteous rebukes administered for doing wrong.

And so it should be, many of you will say. Would we wish a return to be days when children were deported for stealing the loaf of bread that kept them alive? Or we would wish a society like Iran with its *shariah* or Islamic law, which punishes thieves by cutting off their hands?

Surely we should follow the example of Jesus in confronting the woman taken in adultery, who was about to be stoned. Did He not turn the righteous wrath of the crowd back upon themselves and ask those among them who were without sin, to cast the first stone? That shut them up and should it not do the same to we miserable sinners today? Should we not ask ourselves whether the adultress had a bad family upbringing, lacking in love, that she reacts in this way?

Is not the mugger a person who knows only the language of violence through which to express his desperation? These and other rhetorical questions are asked in a spirit of humility with no stones clutched, hidden in the hand. But are they the right questions?

Understanding the minds of those who have enlarged this year's crime statistics is one thing. Punishing them is another. Doing something about their future is yet another. While the Christian spirit with which many view criminals is admirable (turning cheeks, emptying pockets of stones, getting social work reports) and results in increased appreciation of why so many succumb to crime, it is not nearly the whole story.

It deals only with the first stage. It does not face up to the punishment question because it implicitly suggests that they are not culpable if their criminal aetiology can be 'understood'. Yet it is perfectly obvious to anyone who mixes in the real world that they are wicked people who have exercised a choice in favour of the nasty option. They could get money by robbing a fruit machine, but it is easier to beat up an old woman and grab her purse. The rapist could pay a prostitute to satisfy his fantasies but instead he pollutes another human being with his poison body.

At this point some of you suspect that I am about to call for public hanging for pederasts and the boiling in oil of muggers. Well, you would be wrong. I do happen to believe that certain forms of physical punishment could be effective in some cases. (It is paradoxically liberals who provide me with my argument for this when they argue that violent people can be 'understood' since they know no other language with which to express their inarticulate aggro. This being the case we can talk back to them on the same basis and presumably they will understand. OK?)

But most of the time such punishment is wasted because it does not produce repentance or reform. Here is the real area for progress. While the do-goody liberals and the big stick brigade waste their time accusing one another of misunderstanding the criminal mind and argue over the chicken and egg issue of crime and social conditions, the prisons are packed with people who are certainly being punished, but nothing much beyond that.

It is in this area that religion has a role to play. Alongside the excellent chaplaincy work that is done in prisons there are many admirable charities which deal with the care and rehabilitation of offenders. But should the thrust of society as a whole not be directed towards producing a change of heart in criminals?

The fact that this will be seen as an infringement of freedom, a form of brainwashing by the God squad, proves how perverted the situation is. The churches themselves seem occasionally apologetic at best and old fashioned at worst in their missionary efforts.

Yet here is a dark continent on our own doorstep, crying out for missionary endeavour. □

Communion comes but twice a year for some

"EASTER is a time to be joyful, communion is a time to be sad." The elder who spoke those words was opposing the idea of an Easter communion, but unwittingly he was revealing the attitude of a great many Scots Protestants towards the Lord's Supper, the name by which many call communion.

In sombre silence, wearing black ties, the Calvinist elders walk between the unusually-full pews. A floorboard creaks. There is a moment of confusion while one elder fumbles to put his cakestand of individual cups back on the tier. Then the awesome silence is broken by the closing hymn and the congregation skail into the autumn air, all their communion cards safely gathered in, registering their presence and (if Kirk procedure is being properly followed) entered on the roll.

Many kirks hold only two such services in the year, the second at this time of the year. It is inevitable that they are attended by those whose prime motive appears to be to register their attendance and thereby retain their name on the roll. Lest it be thought I am attributing vile motives to such people, it is noticeable that when non-card communions are held, attendance is considerably diminished.

Seasonal tide

Of course the sense of occasion is heightened by this seasonal tide and many feel that here the Calvinist Kirk is at its very essence—grim, taciturn, with the minister perched in judgement on a wicked generation, like a hoodie craw in the pulpit. A further presumption is that the Scots Reformers indulged themselves in communion but twice a year.

Yet all these caricatures are historically misplaced. The Early Church celebrated communion as an *agape* (or Love Feast) with children present. The Greek word *eucharisto* means to rejoice and give thanks, so the Eucharist or communion is hardly a time to be sad. But that is what it has become in many churches where it is surrounded by a po-faced atmosphere akin to a dentist's waiting room.

As for the infrequency with which it is celebrated, this may be thought to be a reaction against the daily sacrifice of the Mass and the emphasis that grace comes dear and difficult not cheap and daily. But here it must be said that John Calvin wanted a weekly communion and the only reason that Knox didn't follow suit in Scotland was the difficulty of organising such events in the rural parishes with a paucity of reformed clergy available to celebrate the sacrament.

So it became a twice-yearly event by necessity, rather than design.

Individual cups

Another hallmark of the modern Protestant communion is the use of individual cups. These little glasses, which so closely resemble eyebaths, have become a fetish, and to suggest that a common cup might be shared (after all it is *communion*) is more than many a minister would dare. Indeed in Lylsland Church in Paisley this fetish was carried so far that even the common cup used by the minister and elders on either side, had three wee individual cups soldered inside the brim, lest their lips should touch. Needless to say they do not practice the kiss of peace there.

This is now part of the Roman Catholic rite, which has never had problems of rampant tuberculosis because of the cup. They (until recently) simply did not give it. They, however, have a wholly different outlook because of transubstantiation, which sounds like a disease but is a doctrine. Effectively it means that the molecules of bread and wine remain unchanged, but their *substance* (a rather shadowy term of Greek philosophy) changes when the actions of the Mass are performed.

High Church Protestants believe there is a spiritual presence at communion which is received with the elements of bread and wine. Low Church Protestants see the ceremony as a memorial—they would argue that Christ is always present with believers and this presence is not deepened by a ceremony and that grace is through faith alone, not ceremonies.

C

Nonetheless there can be great ceremony associated with a Low Church communion. The elements are brought to them, whereas the Episcopalian and the Catholic worshippers have to go forward for theirs.

Supper and sacrament

This is the dichotomy between supper and sacrament, between table and altar. There are further debates engendered by the type of wine used. Fermented, unfermented, and raspberry cordial are sometimes used. Personally I prefer port, and I find it strange that after an example set at Cana, in Galilee, churches persist in changing wine into watered down cordial. One minister I know objected so much, he once declared during the words of institution: "I take these elements of bread and Ribena."

Some churches cater for all tastes. Front pews are common cup fermented, right side is common cup unfermented and so on through all the permutations. Last orders please! Looking across the denominational spectrum we can see that this central act, which is shared by all the major denominations, is celebrated in dozens of different ways and according to dozens of different theological principles. Should we be proud that the loaf broken at the Last Supper is now feeding 5000 denominations in as many different ways?

Perhaps we should not be so ready to sneer at the Close Brethren who deny unbelievers access to their domestic table, when we often do not share our holy table with believers. The Last Supper was not meant to be a Take-Away. □

Cash or credit and muzak, muzak, muzak

THEY'RE all at it. Everywhere you go to shop they have Christmas muzak playing from loudspeakers secreted about the premises. I suppose I should call it Xmas muzak since it has nothing to do with Christ nor with music. It is Andy Williams or James Last billing and cooing. The bland leading the bland.

Or it is a pop group growling their way through a new song with cash register bells providing the timpany. "Have yourself a happy, merry dooby doo beebop tingaling little old Santa sleighbell in the snow dong along teetum yayaya fun among the mistletoe bloop a doop yeh yeh etc, etc."

The temptation to go shopping with a pair of wirecutters and snip the leads to those hidden loudspeakers is immense. Or better still find the source, the cassette player, and rip out the cassette and jump up and down upon it until it is smashed into little pieces.

Have you felt like that? Then spare a thought for the shop assistants who might feel similarly but who have to work alongside this sludge amid the snow, drifting through their ears for hour after hour, freezing their brains into insensible snowballs.

Last week I went into a shop in which Andy Williams was gently exhorting the customers to have a merry, happy, lovely, beautiful, etc,

etc. Eventually a strong urge swept me to do something vandalistic to the apparatus, but I yielded not to temptation and left, returning a couple of hours later to complete my purchases. Andy was still at it. "Have yourself a happy, merry, etc."

A new tactic suggested itself to me. Suppose I joined in and sang the carols along with the cassetted carousers. Would that constitute breach of the peace and goodwill? (Those who have heard me sing will be in no doubt about the outcome.)

It wasn't worth the fine, so I retreated to climb every escalator, dream the impossible dream of a store in which silent night meant peace to shop, and not another glutinous accompaniment to wassailing wallets.

I have visions of some of these poor women who work all day long exposed to such seductive sounds becoming hypnotised. When they stand at the watchnight service and hear those self-same carols they will galvanise into action and begin to take up the offering among the congregation and go off to ring it up on the cash register.

For that is the purpose of the muzak, is it not? It is a variant on the soft sell device of the supermarkets who have apparently demonstrated that people buy more when they are subjected to muzak. What is new is perhaps the idea that people have to be encouraged or influenced to spend.

It used to be accepted that Christmas was a shopping season when people would spend anyway. Now the emphasis has shifted to efforts to help them spend more.

Holders of certain cards are being exhorted in a brochure which accompanies their last statement to take advantage of credit facilities and spread their payments into the new year. Am I alone in questioning the wisdom of giving a gift which the donor cannot afford and which must be paid at the ludicrous interest of 25 per cent or so charged by the credit card companies?

The generosity of the donor must surely be balanced by good sense. Yet how many people this Christmas will be going into debt to pay for the festive season? Too many, I suspect, for their own good.

This is not the Gospel according to Scrooge. The point of that story was that Scrooge could afford to be generous. It was the Cratchet family who could not. Would we commend Bob Cratchet if he had used his credit card to buy his family a lavish Christmas lunch?

Certainly there is Biblical precedent for splashing out on special occasions—Martha's anointing of Jesus with the expensive ointment could easily be used as a justification for spraying around a little champagne to hansel a special occasion.

Killing the fatted calf is another Biblical phrase which ought to act as an antidote to killjoy Christmasses.

Perhaps there is an analogy with holidays. Taking a summer holiday used to be regarded as a luxury that everyone owed to themselves. Then it became a necessity to which nearly everyone conformed. It became an industry in itself and the tourist industry is now acknowledged as an essential part of the Scottish economy.

Christmas must now be an even

greater industry. If spending levels did not escalate at this season then many businesses would go under. Christmas cash keeps the wheels of the economy oiled.

But perhaps the machine has taken over from the individual. The patriarchs of Christmas spending, Santa Claus and Good King Wenceslas, have given way to King Midas. Everything has turned to gold and the inevitable consequence has been to turn individual acts of generosity and compassion into transactions with monetary consequences. There is nothing new in this tendency.

Throughout the Bible there are instances of tribal religion melting their heartfelt yearning for God and transmuting it into idolatory. What greater respect for God than to make an offering of a golden calf? The people who did that were probably well intentioned and did not foresee the consequences.

To save us from ourselves, it is perhaps no coincidence that God chose the humblest and the least affluent circumstances through which to announce Himself. We may spread the bread of life with caviar, and smoke the sides of salmon to toast the fisherman of Galilee, and turn the water into the best claret, but we cannot guarantee He will sit at our table unless we have laid a place for the poor, the outcast, the hungry and the friendless.

For He has warned us that unless we invite them, we will have excluded Him. □

Behind the pot plants, spades are called shovels

The Assemblies of God . . .

IT must surely qualify as ecclesiastical culture-shock to attend the annual assemblies of both Anglicans and Methodists on the same day in different English cities. On this basis I claim the prize/penance/privilege (depending on your prejudice) of so doing. London and Birmingham were the cities. The General Synod of the Church of England and the Methodist Conference were the events; as you expect they are quite different.

The Synod meets at Westminster, just over the road from the Palace of Westminster, and although a relatively modern institution (1970), it has modelled itself on its parliamentary cousins. There are three 'Houses', Bishops, Clergy and Laity (the latter two consisting of elected representatives who serve four years, (the life of the Synod being that of a Parliament). However, they all sit together in the same circular chamber which has various doors marked 'Clergy Ayes' or 'Laity Noes' through which the members of the Synod troop to vote in the way MPs trudge through their voting lobbies.

It is all very low-key and restrained. There are no opposing benches or party whips but unofficial groups like the Anglo-Catholics or Evangelicals meet over lunch to decide tactics. On the opening day a session equivalent to Prime Minister's question time in the Commons enables Synod members to put Church leaders on the spot.

Silly asses

This is when pomposity and pedantry seem to get off the leash. Not so much from the Church leaders but the silly asses who put down world-shattering questions about when the coat of arms of Gibraltar is to be carved on the stonework of Church House alongside other dioceses.

The set-piece debates are usually more interesting, albeit that one gets the impression speakers are carefully sifted in the way that Tory Party conferences ensure that the boat is not rocked too violently.

If the C of E models itself on Parliament, the Methodists model themselves on a school prize-giving. Up on the platform behind a moat of pot plants that would hold back a crowd of football hooligans, sit the Heid Yins flanked by lecterns with large, coloured bulbs. After two minutes of Green, Amber gives another minute, then the unforgivable Red Light. The speeches are short (perhaps the school prize-giving metaphor breaks down at this point) and the polished public school tones of the Synod have given way to nasal northern echoes.

Muck and brass tacks and spades being called shovels. These are the order of the day. Popular and blunt utterances are greeted by cries of "hear, hear," but no applause. Applause is not allowed. But you can say hear, hear as loud as you like.

Print frocks

Methodist men have gold frames on their spectacles. Methodist women wear print frocks. Laughter is permitted, but it is of the glutinous kind which tee hees over in-jokes. Although there are half a million Methodists, there tend to be 50 speakers who dominate proceedings I am told, but the democratic (half ministers—half members) quota means that some circuits can elect seventeen-year-old girls to be their delegates to the conference. (I cannot bring myself to follow the grotesque habit which Methodists seem to have learned from the Labour Party of dropping the definite article and so "Conference does this or that" never "The Conference.")

If the C of E used to be the Tory Party at prayer (and is now the Democrats), the Methodists are the Labour Party at prayer. They also have their equivalent of Militant Tendency known as ARM (Alliance of Radical Methodists). Afterwards I met two of these gentlemen who were exercising their elbows in a nearby hostelry and exercising their right to disagree on conscientious grounds with the Wesleyan distaste for alcholic beverages.

One wore a black felt hat, and his shoulder-length hair and beard were silver enough for him to have known the beatnik era. The other was not a delegate from his circuit of East London since he usually came last in the election (except last year when he was ninth out of eight until a lady delegate became pregnant). These cheerful and middle-aged chaps were the Fringe not the official Festival.

Lukewarm words

They were leaving to eat a curry washed down by whisky from the ex-Jesuit pal upon whose floor they were sleeping. They left my picture of the typical Methodist looking a bit bland. Wouldn't it be nice if there were more surprises like that in all the assemblies of the godly?

Too often they are dominated by smooth committee men in light grey suits with lukewarm words which swill around the mouth like watered-down lemonade. Consensus politics is the game of the mealy-mouthed who are so busy having 'dialogue' with everything that moves that they end up talking a language only they understand, an ecclesiastical esperanto which is alien to the outsider.

All Church assemblies should perhaps have the motto, "Behold I stand at the door and knock" inscribed above the door to remind them that the Church exists for outsiders not insiders. □

Tawdry, insulting concept of God

IT would be a nasty fellow who would kick away someone's crutch. Yet sometimes that is what I feel like doing to the psychological and emotional crutches which are marketed as folk religion. Take the new, improved version of the Cross of Lourdes being advertised in Prediction magazine. The original contained two compartments in which 'genuine' Lourdes water was contained. Now one compartment is filled with earth from Bethlehem. The sleazy sell which accompanies the three-page advert points to those who have been given large sums of money shortly after acquiring their cross. They are presumably twice blessed, having their cake and eating it, with treasure laid up in Heaven and a spot of cash in hand too.

The cross is marketed by Estelit who are part of P.R. Sheridan. They import the crosses from America whither they are taken from France. Among their other talismans is a little Buddha to which the Buddhist Society of Great Britain have apparently taken exception, although the Cross of Lourdes has only attracted five letters of complaint to the magazine since it first was advertised nine months ago.

Enthusiastic

None of these has come from official Church sources, a matter which surprises Mr Demos Strouthos of Prediction magazine, who is enthusiastic in his support of his advertisers. "Morally I see it as strengthening people's faith," he told me.

"Perhaps some people need a psychological or emotional crutch before their faith will come back or to give them more confidence. I've seen myself take something like a rabbit's foot into an interview," says Mr Strouthos.

Although he protests that it is not his job to pass moral judgements on anyone, he does draw the line at advertising some occult products such as polished pebbles, or some cults such as the Moonies. Well, it is a free country isn't it? Mr Strouthos can offer hope to the empty souls and draw his magic circle of exclusion where he wants and the rest of us are free to disbelieve in any or all of his wares.

But is *laissez-faire* the best policy in the free market of religious grottoes? This has been the problem confronting the Catholic hierarchy in countries where devotion to shrines and alleged miracles have got a little out of hand. In Yugoslavia the bishops washed their hands of the apparitions at Medjugorje. The Irish bishops have shown themselves none too keen on the holy sideshow at Ballinspittle where the statue of the Madonna in a grotto allegedly swayed. However, as the busloads of pilgrims trudged up the muddy paths to the whispered prayers ("Our Lady of Ballinspittle sway for us") of the local inn-keepers, the Bishop of Cork gave a lukewarm endorsement to the extent that it was no bad thing to see people praying.

Apparitions

Presumably the Pope felt more confident about giving his blessing to another Irish shrine at Knock whose apparitions have now become world famous and brought an offer from an American company to build an airport there for pilgrims. If Knock is OK and Lourdes is highly commended and the Shroud of Turin is possibly miraculous and the liquefied blood of St Januarius is positive, not negative—then where does the line end? When does holy place become wholly misplaced faith?

Personally I find such debates to be sterile. To me there is no such thing as a holy relic or place. There are places in which one can sense the numinous, the presence of spiritual forces more easily than others. Perhaps it is the beauty of the surroundings, the tradition of stepping in the shoes of countless generations of faithful people. But if God had meant such shrines and grottoes to be the proof for faith in Him, surely He would have taken away our brains. These phenomena are so elusive, so debatable, so exploitable by the credulous and those who thrive on manipulating them that they drive more away from genuine religious experience than they attract to it.

Certainly, there are psychic phenomena. I happen to believe that many of them are very well documented, even proved. But what do they prove? That there are more things in Heaven and Earth than are dreamt of in our understanding. No more than that. You can still believe in ghosts and be an atheist. You can still divine water with a rod and be an agnostic. You can have a vision of tomorrows's air disaster in a dream and be a Christian, a Communist or a Conservative. There is nothing in the event which is necessarily traceable to a divine source and nothing which proves the system of doctrines and revelations that we call religion.

Half-baked faith

It is not because talismans are 'of the devil' that I reject them. It is because they substitute half-baked faith for genuine effort and hold out promises of intervention in the world's affairs on payment. Paying your penny makes God choose you and the idea that God chooses these beggardly talismans as the instruments of His purpose is a cheap, tawdry, insulting and blasphemous concept of God.

It is easy to sneer at the credulous pilgrims. But there is genuine pilgrimage. Most of the Lourdes visitors journey in faith and it is the whole process that becomes a blessing to them. They are not expecting special dispensation and that is why so many of the Lourdes pilgrimages are undertaken by genuine pilgrims who may not be able to throw away their crutches at the end but will find new strength from their visit. On reflection, those who wear emotional crutches need not have them kicked away. They will want to throw them away, when they find mature faith. □

How about an Embassy Woman's Guild meeting

IF you are a celebrity of some kind then the odds are that you have been asked to endorse a product of some kind. If you are a film star and smoke a particular brand of cigar or douse yourself with an exotic perfume then you would be a prime candidate to appear in adverts endorsing these products.

Such seductive selling is not limited to the glossy. Credibility is no respecter of good looks. Beauty is not truth, nor truth beauty. Thus the Metropolitan Commissioner's testimony to a brand of tyre as a major contribution to road safety carries weight because of who he is rather than what he looks like. Or some years ago, if you travelled on Southern Region trains, the tennis star Ann Haydn Jones would beam her endorsement of Biostrath elixir. Anne Packer packed a punch with Baked Beans. Henry Cooper used brute strength to promote after-shave.

Needless to say I have not been asked to endorse anything. The fact that S. J. Lamont smokes Dobies Number 7 mixture is hardly likely to start a rush on tobacconists for this particular weed. (Would that it did, for there are many shops who pretentiously call themselves tobacconists but who stock a meagre number of vulgar brands.)

Haughtily I will now declare that even if asked I could not endorse anything in which I did not believe. For there is an ugly rumour that some of these film stars and sports personalities do not really use the products which they advertise.

Foot balm

My own taste is so eclectic (or should I say conditioned by the cheapest bargain available) that I am not evangelical on behalf of any product—except perhaps Valpeda foot balm, which soothes the weary feet better than anything I know, softens hard skin and banishes athlete's foot. Can anyone ask for more?

Perhaps one day there will be an advert using Biblical images, the footsore traveller will be seen having his feet anointed (for which there is excellent Scriptural precedent) and softly the music will steal up in the background—and it will be Handel's 'How beautiful are the feet'.

This testimony approach is the stuff of applied evangelism. But it is not the only approach by which the message is put over. Sponsorship is a new and benevolent way of accruing goodwill and custom.

The manufacturer's name is blazoned across an event of worthwhile significance. The Hitachi Highland Games or the Peter Stuyvesant Alpine Ski Championship or the Embassy World Snooker Championship. Perhaps it is hoped that the interest or pleasure generated by the event will be transferred mentally to the product name.

Now it seems to me that the Churches have a great deal to gain from this method of selling their message. Some of the evangelical churches know this already and have large banners proclaiming 'Jesus Saves'. But they often make the mistake of putting them up at crusades when they are only likely to be preaching their simple message to the converted. Perhaps a few adverts round the football terraces would spread the net a little wider.

The organisers of the Papal Mass at Bellahouston are likely to have a far bigger crowd than any football ground, and if the television audience is added then the potential is almost unlimited. The McCormick organisation has not been slow to seize on this fact and in future one might suppose that the Hierarchy will have learned from this. They may make use of the brevity of Latin tags, just as pithy as any adman's lingo. Imagine a banner round Parkhead, '*Extra ecclesiam non salus est*'.

Raised banners

And what about the General Assembly of the Church of Scotland, I wonder if they too could make use of this method of selling their wares? As the television cameras skim the ranks of ministers and elders, perhaps the odd banner might be raised reading '*reformata sed semper reformanda*'.

Maybe the sponsorship option ought to be considered as a solution to the Kirk's financial plight. What about the Peter Stuyvesant General Assembly of the Church of Scotland? Or the Embassy Woman's Guild Annual Meeting? If the tobacco road is considered the one-way street to perdition, then let me say that it is as incompatible as the marriage of athletic sports with smoking sponsorship. They could always put up a banner, '*mens sana in corpore sano*'.

That might be the motto of the Scottish Health Education Group who not only advertise on television but sponsor a radio soap opera, to say nothing of the Scottish football team. If we accept that it is reasonable for Health to sell its message in this way, why are we wary of religion? Or is it just that Health comes under the national budget but religion is considered to be propaganda? How ironic. ☐

Suffering the little children

NEVER appear with animals or children, says the showbiz adage, but it might have been addressed to clergymen as well as actors. Certainly there is little danger of a minister having to share the pulpit with a dog, although I must confess that my very own canine friend has pretensions to being a biped.

I have christened her the Blessed Dawg and her large brown eyes are filled with sorrowful compassion, her wrinkled forehead, which was bequeathed by her bloodhound ancestors, is the very epitome of worried concern. Such expressions would fittingly accompany many a sermon and when stricken with a sore throat I

have been tempted to invite the Blessed Dawg to assume her two-legged stance within the pulpit, in my stead.

There she would stand conveying the burden of being a creature and the sorrow to which humanity (but more so caninity) is heir to. That old smarty pants Dr Samuel Johnson was fond of saying that a woman preaching was like a dog standing on hind legs—it was not done well but it was surprising to find it done at all. Behold, I could show him a new thing.

However, my tale is not of legs and the man. It is of children in church, or bairns in the kirk. Nowhere is the showbiz adage more true than here. Numberless are the ministers who have come to grief at the height of their peroration as a child has let out a deep sigh, articulating the inner feelings of some and distracting into amusement the rest of the congregation who were listening.

A mighty fall

When, during the Children's Address, a rhetorical question is asked as a step towards drawing the moral at the end, there is great danger of a mighty fall. "Do you know what a vestry is, children?" asked a friend of mine, probably hoping that none of them did. (In children's addresses the minister has the last word or more often The Correct Answer.) On this occasion he had not allowed for his four-year-old son Robert, who piped up: "The vestry is where Daddy does the toilet before the service." My friend, whose ablutions are an elaborate, and to him, essential part of his pre-sermon warm up, was for once lost for words.

Much less amusing is the mewling infant. (I miss out the word puking from this Shakespearean phrase since I know of few instances in which a baby has strained the cassock of the clergyman baptising it, though doubtless readers may know of one.) I remember the smiles of delight which spread across the face of one mother when the little fleshly alarm clock which I had been handed, went off at the crucial moment. It was the kind of grin on the face of a leather-jacketed youth when he revs his motor bike and watches the grimaces on the faces of those standing around. In this case the grimace was on the face of the rev.

A worse incident happened to me when invited to preach at a special service in a small church which was well filled for the occasion. I had been asked for a full text of the sermon, to be printed in the society minutes and had gone to some trouble to prepare for the occasion.

In the corner of the church was a visiting group of Guides whose camp was nearby, and on the knees of one Guider was an infant which kept up a constant (and unchecked by her) chatter throughout the readings and prayers. I knew then that I had walked into a situation from which there would be no escape. I rose to preach with a jolly remark about there being an official opposition, "but perhaps it will be going for a walk in a little while". (HINT HINT.)

Two minutes later I could hardly hear myself, so I smiled (less warmly, I admit) and suggested that the time had come for walkies. There was an awkward pause during which it became clear that this hint was going to be ignored like all previous ones and then the Guider realised that the pause was going to continue. She left.

Not enthralled

The bolt of lightening did not come until a week later. If it was not on asbestos paper it should have been. A cup of foaming vitriol had been prepared for my anointing by the infant's grandmother, who was the mother of the Guider and a member of the church although not present on this occasion. Had she been, she informed me, she would have protested there and then. (Who said church services were always dull?)

This unfortunate episode allows several points to be made about children in church.

The first is a good motto: when in doubt, take them out. The second is that children who are used to watching Going Live are not likely to be enthralled by the Black and White Minister Show. The third is that if the easy way out is taken and the children stay away, then the church will be deprived of their fresh and youthful presence. Not only will the ranks of its future membership suffer, but the impression will be conveyed that what is done in church is For Adults Only.

Sadly, there are many people who say that the Children's Address is what speaks to them, rather than other parts of a Protestant service. This may be due to the poor quality of the preaching or it may be due to the fact that some Christians have their own interpretation of the dominical saying, "Except ye be as little children ye cannot enter the kingdom of heaven".

Their understanding of their faith has not changed since they quit Sunday School and their insights are childish, not child-like. When Paul says: "When I became a man I put away the things of children", he does not mean rejecting the innocence, the sparkle and the insights of youth. The advice to grow in faith, hope and love refers to an increase in quality, not quantity. □

Gospel according to Hollywood

VIOLENCE begets violence. The cliche is never more true than in the black and white morality of the technicolour red-blooded Western movie. The baddies perpetrate dirty deeds. Some goodies are gunned down. Enter the Hero, who then fights it out with the baddies. They bite the dust with lead in their bellies.

This scenario has been repeated time and time again from Stagecoach and High Noon through the fast food diet of the Lone Ranger (plus Tonto) and the Range Rider (plus Dick West—all American boy). There was even solid, respectable-like Bonanza whose heroes were like unto Saints. Then came the day of the anti-hero.

Westerns got mean and dirtier. Baddies and goodies became less distinguishable from one another. The Magnificent Seven, a bunch of hard, gun-slinging thugs, were the heroes of the movie. The logical development of this was a film in which there were no heroes, only victims and violence. Soldier Blue was it. The nadir had been reached.

It was the end of an era. The Western movie had been to America, the new promised land, what the Old Testament and its heroes—Abraham, Moses, Samson, Saul and David—had been in Biblical times. At least that is what I took out of them. There was the same mission to conquer land with gold replacing milk and honey, a wagon-train exodus, a plethora of heroes with a policy of taking an eye for an eye and a tooth for a tooth. Above all, God was on their side.

This Old Testament of the West has been up-dated. The frontiersman heroes such as Davy Crockett no longer excite our moral support. The massacre of the Alamo is less audience-grabbing than a Vietnam village scorched in napalm. So the old wine is being poured into new bottles.

Rough justice

The new heroes are bright young CIA-types who clean up the baddies in the Establishment, or journalists who oppose the abuse of political power, or expose nuclear power policy. These are the new improved, biological, whiter than white heroes.

But the appetite for rough justice which the gun-toting sheriff satisfied does not easily go away. The all-American cop is his successor.

Whether exposing a bent cop in the system, comforting the widow of a colleague, or shooting it out with drug peddlers in downtown LA, he administered the convenant in Gun Law. The original Marshal Dillon, James Arness, returned in such a role. Even Captain Kirk has stopped pushing back the frontiers of the universe boldly to go on to the streets as a cop with the unlikely name of Hooker, a case of Starsky being put into a hutch.

It's all good clean fun. We had our own British equivalent in The Professionals and The Sweeney which added our apocrypha to the Gospel according to Hollywood. But one facet of the Wild West which has never been part of our social scene is surfacing now in cinematographic form. He is the vigilante.

Vigilantes were the self-appointed administrators of justice and public executioners. At worse they were a lynch mob. But the vigilante is now a film hero played by Charles Bronson. His wife and daughter were mugged and raped and he set out on a trail of revenge killings in cold blood, making himself bait for the muggers. But it is bait which hit back with bullets.

The vigilante's cousin is Dirty Harry, the cop hero played by Clint Eastwood who also typifies the evolution from old to new celluloid.

In the film Magnum Force he ironically blasts away a set of cops who have become off duty vigilantes. A sequel apparently has an even higher body count.

The violence of these movies is sometimes excused on the ground that they portray violence already existing in society or that they entertain. These reasons do not justify the righteous role which they assign to the avenging vigilante. In many ways the amoral blood baths were preferable because they made no such pretence. Of course, we do not have to enjoy them.

Dangerous

But it is precisely because many of us do that they are dangerous. Which of us on finding our car aerial snapped off by a vandal have not momentarily wanted to do the same to his neck? I am not ashamed to admit that I am not overwhelmed with sympathy for muggers and molesters. The vigilante movie plays to those emotions in all of us, legitimising it.

It would be smug to imagine that all such violence is across the Atlantic. There are enough horror stories of rape, murder and robbery in our own society to warrant the assumption that the burglar in our bedroom is not likely to be Raffles the gentleman crook.

But if we are intruded upon what should we do? Should we be passive and possibly die from lack of self defence—or shoot him dead and be tried for culpable homicide? It is hardly likely that a vicious thug will wait politely while we ring the police.

The difference could be one of life or death. But it is also a difference of a fundamental nature, similar to that between Old and New Testaments. The former is an accurate insight to where we are, the latter into where we ought to be. As such it means that vigilante heroes, no matter how good, are not the stuff of which Christians are made.

The last word does not always go to

the fastest gun. Possibly the most poignant illustration of that was from the last testament of the Assistant Governor of the Maze Prison, "I feel sorry for them," he said of his killers, knowing as he wrote that he was likely to die. Surely the nobility of his words speaks louder than the guns of vengeance. □

An even sadder side to epitaphs

'GOD had a space in his garden, so He took our Uncle Ted.' This sad epitaph appeared in a newspaper which I picked up, under the In Memoriam notices. It is sad in several ways, not just because it springs from genuine human grief but because poor Uncle Ted, no matter how theologically illiterate he may have been, deserves better.

I am sure that the people who inserted the notice had the best of motives. But did they realise that in trying to staunch the bleeding heart, they had administered a tourniquet to the artery of free will? The God who would pluck a thousand Uncle Teds to fill his heavenly vase is a monster. But one that we have created by attributing a secret and higher purpose to a tragic event. God is not a puppeteer who controls us, otherwise a great deal of moral purpose would

vanish from life, nor is the apprenticeship of suffering something which is willed upon us.

If the universe was created with bricks and mortar and free-will, then someone somewhere is bound to drop a free-falling brick on someone else's toe. And there will be fatal accidents and disease. And although it may smack of determinism, there will be certain laws that if a brick or apple is dropped, they will fall to the ground, the latter getting bruised. That is in the nature of things.

So much for Uncle Ted dying of natural causes. There remains for me a disturbing element about In Memoriam notices. I have no wish to intrude my feelings upon the many bereaved people who insert such notices, but I ask myself—why do they invite me to intrude upon their private grief by inserting the notice in that most public of places, the newspaper? Perhaps they wish to share their grief, but if I did not know Uncle Ted, then it becomes less easy to sympathise. By being publicly mourned he who was anonymous becomes blatantly famous.

There is another reason and it is supplied by scanning the Memorial notices in a Catholic newspaper. After the letters R.I.P. there is often the phrase "St Theresa pray for him. . . ." The implication that St Theresa reads the Scottish Catholic Observer is perhaps mischievous on my part, but it does raise the question of why the petition was not addressed to the saint directly and required publication to make it more efficacious. The reason may be that all who knew the deceased are thus reminded of him and are invited to pray for his repose (through St Theresa or otherwise).

Continuity

We have stumbled now into the dark cellars of ecumenism whence multilateral Church conversationalists dare not go. For deep in the vaults of Protestant Kirks there are no altars to the dead and no prayers to them or for them. They are beyond earthly intercession and in the everlasting arms of God. To offer such intercession is considered at least a presumption and at worst occultist, using the magic of candles.

To the Catholic it is perfectly straightforward, springing from belief in the survival of bodily death and the continuity between this world and the next. It is only an extension of care for the individual in this life to continue to express concern after death. Posthumous birthday and get well cards are therefore understandable if you take this view. Having a saint handle the message or provide a heavenly *poste restante* seems therefore a wise precaution—for, as Catholics continually have to point out to unsympathetic Protestants, the saint is an agent furthering prayer, not its recipient.

But it is not always Catholics who insert In Memoriam notices in the paper. These notices are sometimes the only way the agnostic or the non-church member can find of expressing their grief. Possessing no ecclesiastic franchise, they expiate their grief by posting an In Memoriam notice. Sadly they probably do not know much of the Bible and have few friends among the saints, so they opt for one of the little poems which some

newspapers have on offer in a little book. These are seldom from Shakespeare or Keats, Eliot or Auden. Instead I am convinced they are done by those literary graffiti artists who compose the rhymes in Christmas cards and are executed in a state of tired insobriety and cynicism on new year's morning.

My grandfather was a pillar of the Kirk, a gentle man with a pawky wit, and it used to amuse him to read aloud these rhymes to my Granny, exhorting her to choose one for him. One daily paper provides plenty of stomach-turning examples:

It's not the tears that fall at the time,
That tell of the heart that is broken,
It's the lonely tears in the after years,
When my dad's name is spoken.
Lord put your arms around him,
Treat him with special care,
Make up for all he suffered,
And all that was unfair.

Despite the vulgar character of such poetry it conceals a genuine sadness. That is why it disgusts me to see the nobility of grief caricatured in this way. It has its funny side but ultimately it is about sadness.

The deep-rooted need to express grief is part of all religions and perhaps the Protestant churches should see these notices as a cry for help. To provide a place within your tradition where a candle may be lit, not for magic but for memory, its flickering flame symbolising the frailty of human life, its warmth communicating the mercy of God's love, its light illuminating the dark night of despair.

Perhaps it is right that faith should not need its followers to pray for the dead ... "Let the dead bury their dead." Yet there will always be those whose love for Uncle Ted, now deceased, looms so large that their grief overwhelms their faith. It is here that hope has a place. The candle of hope is to me a more satisfactory symbol than a sickly stanza. □

Men of the moustache

THE ecclesiastical moustache is an odd divider of denominations. It is far more frequently found upon the upperlips of Kirk ministers than those of Catholic priests. Indeed the identi-kit minister called 'God's man' used to appear on the back cover of Life and Work in advertisements inviting legacies to be left to the Church and Ministry department, was aged about 60 and had white hair and a moustache.

It was a fair archetype, representative not only of the average minister in age, but typical of many in appearance. Among that most representative breed of ministers, Moderators, it is even closer to the mark, and without consulting the records I can think of the Very Reverends MacLeod, Fraser, Craig (Archie), Craig (Robert) and Reid, as examples. The close connections between many padres and the Army has left its shape in the form of the moustache sported by such ministers. It is decidedly Army in shape. For an RAF (and raffish) moustache more recently we are

grateful to Dr Shaw. Whereas ex-SAS padre Dr McLuskey wore his facial hair on his eyebrows.

The Latin origins of the Roman Catholic Church would have dictated a very different shape of moustache and this is perhaps why priests are not permitted to sport this form of decoration.

The Latin moustache is the kind worn by the lounge lizard in the movies. Clark Gable, Errol Flynn, Adolph Menjou—these are not the kind of men to serve as archetypes for celibate priests. They are menacingly sexual with their slick moustaches and one is never sure whether these types will treat their women properly. It is all too easy to spot the cad on vintage silver screens. He is the one with the Latin moustache.

Strong objector

This Roman Catholic prohibition does not extend to Anglicans, but the High Church party have trimmed accordingly. In 1860, the last bishop to wear his wig to the House of Lords died, and his successor as Bishop of Rochester, Dr Joseph Wigram, sharply criticised the wearing of beards and moustaches by the clergy.

In 1891 the point was severely reiterated by Dr Maclagan, the Archbishop of York, who was a strong objector to moustaches despite having been a major in the Madras cavalry and who walked "as though he had his loins girded by a sword belt".

In 1928, when Cosmo Lang was made Archbishop of Canterbury and went for his first royal audience, the King remarked that he hoped he would stop the clergy wearing moustaches. The same inhibitions which kept clergy clean-shaven seem to have applied to clerical uniform.

Although the dog-collar is but an innovation of a mere 100 years antiquity, the wearing of robes are more venerable. The Geneva gown cloaks its wearer not only with respectability and the aura of scholarly authority, but serves to emasculate his physique.

Even more successful in this purpose is the white surplice which happily hangs from Anglican shoulders. Unless, of course, the shoulders are those of the Presbyterian minister who took holiday relief for an Anglican cousin. The vicar insisted that it would mean wearing the uniform his people would recognise, and that included the surplice. On return from holiday he enquired how the strange ecclesiastical garb had suited his friend. "Not too bad," came the reply, "but I was glad to get that surplice off and get my trousers back on again."

Gaiters, you would imagine, would have been banned years ago, as they enable the dashing bishop to show a leg in its full shape. Of course the converse can be said, as several knobbly and bow-legged clerics would humbly be the first to acknowledge.

"Black gaiters and breeches are not dignified, not cheap and not practicable," said George Reindrop, the recent Bishop of Guildford. "A quite archaic outfit," said the Bishop of Crediton, "and the worst possible thing for praying in. The knees go so quickly." The Bishop of Kensington declared, "Gaiters stopped being any use when bishops gave up riding horses as their mode of transport."

But a more novel objection came from Dr Leonard Wilson, when Bishop of Birmingham, and who opened a school without wearing gaiters as a form of protest because he believed: "Bishops should not dress up in the way of the decadent eighteenth century."

Swollen heads

The other side of the gaiter was evidenced by Archbishop William Temple who found them "the most comfortable leg coverings I have ever worn". One of his successors, Lord Fisher, explained that gaiters were for the restriction of blood circulation and possibly accounted for the number of swollen heads among their wearers, but he added that, "I myself find them a very comfortable kind of bondage".

Nowadays it would be considered kinky indeed for a Catholic priest to acquire a tonsure at the hairdressers—or to parade around in soutane and biretta. These are as out of fashion as boned corsets or shoulder pads. I nearly said as pencil skirts, but these have had a revival recently. Ecclesiastical fashion is slower in its cycles of change, but after the short sleeves and jeans of Vatican II have worn thin, I would not be surprised to see a few fedoras perched on the heads of priests—perhaps even with a drooping moustache. Father Zorro!

Let it not be thought this will exclude the Presbyterians who are already making secret trips to Roman Catholic outfitters and coming away with bright blue cassocks and nifty black shirts with priestly collars which can be removed in the twinkling of an eye. These will be handy when they need to put on the pink tie to go to the youth club disco.

Moderators still continue to wear the gaiters and lace when there is no rule to say they must. Do not be misled by thinking that this is either because of strict conformity or regulations laid down. Like many in the entertainment business, they love dressing up. It's all good clean shaven fun. □

Lessons to be learned from three decades of horror

HORROR movies have changed a lot in recent years. When I was a young lad in the 'fifties, the foreboding 'X' certificate was awarded to films which showed people in bed together or—and these were the ones I wanted to see—the Mummy, the Werewolf, Dracula, and good old Frankenstein. Far from being terrifying, I always felt these pleasant films were cheerful and harmless.

Unless you were of 'a nervous disposition' (what a lovely genteel phrase that is) you were unlikely to be distressed by these tales of goodies versus the bad monsters, especially as the goodies always won in the end.

Although, to keep the fun going, Dracula was resurrected as was the Mummy, or Frankenstein's grandson tried do-it-yourself monster-making with the inevitably horrible results.

Seeing these movies now in a late-night television slot only confirms how harmless they all are. They are (relative to most other material) suitable for children, and there has even been 'The Munsters' comedy serial which exploits the fun side of horror movies.

By the time I was old enough to be officially admitted to 'X' certificate performances the 'sixties had dawned and La Dolce Vita. Foreign films full of dark silences punctuated by the occasional grunt and heavy breathing had become 'classics of the cinema'. Earnest young poseurs deemed them to be art and the rest of us were bored silly. To be horrified—surely the purpose of the horror movie—we had to be content with films about psychopathic killers who lurked in bushes or deserted mansions.

Truly horrific

The 'seventies saw a tidal wave of supernatural horrors featuring demonic possession, poltergeists, and various manifestations of the Great Beast. These were truly horrific. However, by this time I had outgrown my adolescent appetite for being shocked and had acquired some knowledge of parapsychology.

Thus I was only too aware that the realities of psychic phenomena were somewhat exaggerated by these treatments. Poltergeists were as likely to depart from a house because of cheap and cheerful methods such as gentle pastoral counselling, as the religious fire brigade scooshing holy water and waving crucifixes.

What is worse, the 'sixties had not resulted in a spate of psychopathic killers trying to emulate the movies, but films like 'The Exorcist' resulted in many people imagining they were possessed.

They were encouraged in this delusion by publicity for films like 'The Amityville Horror' and 'The Entity' which claims that these were based on true stories. There may have been a grain of truth in this, and indeed the symptoms suffered by many people were real enough, but it was question-begging in the extreme to say that the states of mind induced were due to evil forces.

In one way these three decades of horror provide a parable of how we try to explain evil in humanity. The first is the animal, the bestial, which has played a part in symbolising occult and malevolent forces throughout history. We still talk of yielding to animal passions.

Evil actions

The second explanation is that of sick and diseased minds who produce evil by their actions. The third explanation is that psychic power for good or evil is contained in each mind and that certain conditions can unlock it, with sometimes frightening results. There is an element of truth in all of these.

We should not forget our animal origins or our brain's capacity to malfunction or the hidden potential of the unconscious mind. They can all help us in understanding conduct which seems to degrade humanity. Perhaps they are at their most dangerous when possessed by someone with the gift of persuasive speech and power and influence.

Movie myth

But that does mean that we accept the movie myth that these forces are externalised or become absolute in some creatures or people. They cannot be distilled in pure form. They are more like shadows in the forest which enable us to see the contour of the trees to bring them together as the forces of darkness is to obliterate both the wood and the trees.

It is an age-old heresy to see the world as a battleground between the forces of good and evil. But in times of uncertainty a clear division of black and white seems comforting. You pick your side and fight for it.

The only trouble with this tendency is that polarisation occurs. Grey becomes black and white. Amoral becomes immoral.

The language of rhetoric becomes the substitute for argument. If you want an illustration of that you only have to look at the words of President Reagan. Like a character in one of those horror movies he once intoned: "Peace does not come from weakness. Peace comes from strength." Tell that to the Prince of Peace, who hung upon the cross because of the forces of evil. Crucified among thieves, he chose the way which reconciled the forces of light and darkness.   □

Gambling, grace, and greed

THE heads of the devotees are bowed reverently. The officiant's sepulchral tones waft out into the darkened hall. Suddenly, like a hallelujah bursting from a revivalist meeting, a cry rends the air. "House!"

Another day of devotions at the bingo hall are ended and with a suitable benediction in their ears, the players skail into the night air—or even afternoon sunshine, for this religion is no once-a-week affair, but the game the whole family can play all day long, all the week round.

It has claimed many converts. A land that once flowed with cinemas and theatres, now resounds to the clickety-click of another beat. Those who are called according to its rules are justified by their reward. Those who have been rewarded, call out their justification. For here is played the parable of predestination, here the inherent changes and chances of life are put into focus.

The great voice which calls us all has appointed that one card will remain blank and another shall be full, and not for any good or well they've done to him. For the failure, there is always another chance to redeem himself, with another card, another game, at a price, of course.

That is where the little parable breaks down. Grace is free, bingo is not. And unless someone possesses

unique powers of extrasensory perception which enables him to influence the balls in the caller's cabinet, character references are strictly irrelevant to the outcome of the jolly game of life in which eyes look down rather than upward for support.

The basis of the traditional antipathy of churches to gambling is that it can encourage greed, become addictive and is looking for a reward that has not been earned either by virtue or by effort.

No temptation

Thus, persistent gambling or the squandering of large sums of money upon it has been regarded as a sin. Let he who is without sin cast the first stone, I may be hearing you say. In this regard I can boast a kind of virtue, in that I do not gamble. However, lest you think that I am too good to be true, let me at once add that I am not in the slightest inclined to gamble. There is thus no temptation resisted and therefore no virtue gained.

Indeed my reasons for not finding gambling 'attractive' are not the most admirable either. I know there are such things as odds and that they are seldom in my favour. The more I bet, the more I increase the probability of the bookie making the profit (or the bingo hall).

I adduce as evidence for this statement the standard of living enjoyed by bookmakers, bingo hall proprietors, and gaming machine operators. (Have you seen an unemployed bookie?) These two armed bandits do not steal their ill-gotten gains. People give them money.

That is why I cannot find it within me to sympathise with the poor punters who once besieged the offices of the Daily Mail demanding their £35,000 in prize money only to find that when the music stopped there were more winners than chairs for them to sit upon.

It serves them right for playing a game in which even the winners become losers if they try to repeat their success. As inexorable as gravity brings the high jumper back to earth, so doth the winnings of the gambler return unto him who gave them.

I find newspaper bingo even more repulsive than the cinema-hall type, because it encourages people to read newspapers for the wrong reason. We scoff at the pretentious person who buys the Tatler to exhibit it on the coffee table, so why should we not view with less than admiration the newspaper which bribes its readers to buy it for reasons other than its content?

The Mail began bingo as an answer to the bingo weapons of the Daily Star and the Sun in their circulation war and they dignified it with the name 'Casino', but a heap of dung by any other name still smells the same.

Low profile

Usually campaigns against gambling are the prerogative of the fiercer Protestant denominations. Organisations such as Gamblers Anonymous concern themselves with piecing together the casualties of addiction. The latter assumes a low profile and concentrates on the pastoral approach. The former can easily be caricatured as humourless puritans who object to games which involve guessing the number of beans in a jar at the church fete.

But the puritan lobby do a disservice to their cause by lumping everything under the one name, just as the temperance lobby forfeit respect by classing a Christmas sherry with a vodka bacchanal.

Casinos are the wine bars of the gambling world. Bookies are the spirits, the tots of rum. Whereas, bingo is the beer hall of the gambling world. As for church raffles, football club sweeps and fairground tombola, they are fizzy lemonade in comparison and football pools have always seemed to me as harmless as the Christmas sherry.

Indeed none of these things is immoral in itself, but the degree of time and money we spend on them is surely the key. Some of them offer the beguiling idea that skill can influence the odds in our favour, but acquiring that skill usually means spending more time and money.

Bingo, played in a newspaper or otherwise, involves no skill, no moral quality, only large quantities of money and people to make it successful. As such it is the very antithesis of religion. Marx once described religion as the "opium of the people". I wonder if he would now agree that *bingo* is the opium of the people. □

It's humbug! And pass me the soor plooms

A MINISTER friend of mine says he prefers the version of the Christmas story written in the Gospel of Mark. This is his acid way of counteracting the Alka-Seltzer effervescence which is washing about the stomach at this time of year.

As those versed in the Bible will know, the Gospel of Mark begins at the Temptations and contains no mention whatever of the birth of Jesus. It is as if those prologues to the Gospels of Matthew and Luke had not been written. They are the great Temptation in themselves, for they present a Messiah whose credentials are established by miracle. They are the 'magic' of Christmas.

To deny this magic is to incur the wrath of a great number of people. There are those who sincerely believe that this portion of scripture with wise men, virgin birth and a star has the authentic stamp of history upon it. There are others who are not too worried about that, but who crave a good time. They are happy to suspend disbelief for the season of goodwill and lustily to bawl out the carols with beery breath and watch dewy-eyed as the little ones do their stuff.

There seems to be rather a lot of the latter about, if those astute fellows,

the marketing and advertising men, are anything to go by. These wily chaps have realised that goodwill means having to show it. That means a present or at the very least a card for people you know. And of course it would be meanness to pop your neighbour's through the letter box, so it must be sent by mail.

Churlish indeed the man who wishes his neighbour a Merry Christmas but does not give him tangible proof of this to put on his mantlepiece. It is not about sincerity, so much as being seen to be sincere.

But it would spoil the illusion if all the merrymakers were to think that their spending bonanza was for their own satisfaction. That would be selfish and thus it is necessary to encourage them as they wheel their trolleys round the glittering supermarkets, by the playing of Christmas carols.

These must not be sung in the unfamiliar acoustic of the Church hymn, but suitably doctored so that they do not make shoppers stop their trolleys to listen. They must be arranged like the background smooch music of a romantic movie to create atmosphere, hinting at a tune but never arresting the attention. Hence Cliff Richard's producers once produced a clever beaty version of 'Little Town of Bethleham' and The Royal Tank Regiment band had a dreamy pipe band rendering of 'See Amid the Winter Snow,' which I liked to think of as 'Bagpipes over Bethlehem'.

Pop carols, of course, mustn't create the unfortunate habit of diverting attention to the figure of Jesus. Thus the genius of songwriters has been brought to bear on writing a gospel more suited to our age when a baby is born with a plastic spoon in its mouth. Flesh dollies like Sheri Dean and the Sobell Skaters brought out a disc entitled 'Make Someone Happy (this Christmas)' which exhorted us to "spread the word and light the lights, can't you feel the town is bright?"

Another group called Pendulum sang of "White Confetti ... see it falling, bless the stranger in the manger ... in the morning when Christianitee was born". Note the more overt reference to religion but careful avoidance of Jesus Christ which is rather too religious a term. The Johnny Mathis 'A Child is Born' disc also avoided this by fudging the identity of the infant—"The world is waiting for one child ... black, white, yellow? ... no one knows." The black keeps the race relations lobby happy, but can this be a detail we missed hitherto—a yellow Jesus?

No one could possibly take exception to this Mathis infant. No one except someone like Mr Scrooge, the famous Dickens character who used to exclaim "Christmas! Bah! Humbug!", but whose heart was melted by the poor family of Bob Cratchet. Yet not before he had been thoroughly frightened by the ghosts who warned him of terrible judgment.

Still, there is plenty to justify Scrooge's charge of humbug in our present day Christmas practice, and I sometimes wonder if it is us who need to be frightened out of our effervescent joy. Does one have to be a Scrooge to by cynical about pleasures which are derived from escaping reality rather than embracing it? Does one have to be a spoilsport by suggesting that much of the three-line whippery which corrals family groups together is false jollity?

The participants are often quarrelling before the day is out, their only consolation being that they have not been left out in the cold. If we were honest we would admit that every family has such a diplomatic problem. Christmas creates loneliness by creating the appearance of togetherness.

At the root of my disgust is not rampant misanthropy, despite the ample evidence which can be adduced for the evils of humankind. They remain undiminished by all the Christmas cheer. Bombs still go off, children starve to death and people are imprisoned for their thoughts, not their crimes. What is so sad is that through all the tinsel shines a reality, but we cannot seem to grasp it. So we make it all up and pretend it's true.

Remember those soldiers who stopped fighting the Great War to play football across the Flanders trenches and exchange sweeties? They resumed hostilities the next day. Just like the rest of us. Have a humbug! Pass the soor plooms. □

SPIRIT

The finer feelings, by which we know God...

God forgive us for the vipers in our midst

1981—the year which saw the attempted assassinations of President Reagan and Pope John Paul. John Lennon and President Sadat were not so fortunate . . .

THE poison is everywhere. This generation of vipers has again bitten one of the hands that was stretched out in blessing it. In Atlanta the score of young blacks who have disappeared join the unlucky 13 women from Yorkshire in swelling the total. The man who gave the world songs of peace and love died this year in the stench of gunsmoke. The Rancher President, who had carried a gun for the sake of the movie camera, nearly perished by the gun. Now the poison has struck again and the world prays for the Man of Prayer.

The shooting of the Pope has united millions in prayer. He is not just the Pope of the Roman Catholics but a symbol of human beings striving to create institutions and practices which bring them closer to the ways of God. But the best-laid schemes of mankind and its security police can be blown aside in the squeeze of the assassin's trigger, sending one to heaven and one to hell and not for any good or ill they've done to him. The insanity of one unites the sane majority, while the ghoul and the cynic get another cheap thrill.

Painful truth

The stunned emotions and the heartfelt sympathy can obscure a painful truth. We who are brought together by such an obscene act, like to think of ourselves as the vast majority. If we are, then our democracy is ruled by unclean spirits. Who have been the faces on the front pages of the newspapers this week? Who but the Terrorist, the Ripper and the would-be Assassin. Perhaps they and their legions are really in control, receiving their recruits from the unclean spirits in all of us.

83

Frustration, rage, bitterness, fear, despair, hate, envy, lust, pride—always in plentiful supply where human beings settled throughout the globe, but never so much in supply as in the present age of mass psychosis. They are our emotions. Our collective unconscious does not dream Martin Luther King's dream, or pray Pope John Paul's prayer, it endures the nightmare of the lost souls, the raving of the unclean spirit. Send not to know by whom the trigger is squeezed, it is squeezed by us all. May God forgive us for the age in which we live.

Love is a four-letter word. Peace has five letters and two fingers outstretched in a sign whose reverse is obscene. Peace and Love, the cliche of the 'sixties, has again become soiled by the paraffin stains on the hands that hold an assassin's gun.

The Nobel Peace Prize winner lies ignoble and dead upon the lone and level sands of Egypt. "Look on my works, ye mighty and despair." We must all despair that once again the bullet has triumphed over the brain. Is it not a telling comment on our times that to preach peace is to invite violence upon your person?

Martin Luther King was another winner of the Peace Prize. Prizes do not matter, but what he did was supremely important in calming the racial tensions of America in the 'sixties.

The Swinging 'Sixties, Peace and Love and the Beatles go together like a horse and carriage. All you need is love—the requiem for John Lennon, prophet of peace who met a similar fate. All three people died for different reasons, if it is not absurd to associate the word reason with the hateful and cowardly acts which killed them. They were all associated with Peace in different ways but a different type of peace in each case. Love has four letters and four meanings, and peace has two faces, two edges when the sword is beaten into a ploughshare.

Dynamic

There is the peace of the graveyard, dead and inert. It is frozen and passive. Then there is the peace of the fast-flowing river, dynamic and active. One is life-giving and the other is measured by the absence of life. There is the negative peace of a phoney war or a balance of power, which is not peace at all.

The peace which is on the face of a sleeping child is not the same as the peace on a face whose eyes are closed in prayer. To say this is not to play with words but to assert there is more to peace than a word with five letters. There is action.

Lennon's devotion to the world of transcendental meditation may have brought him inner peace, but it remained locked behind the doors of his perception until he sang about it. Peace is not something experienced, but shared. It has a social dimension, which the Hebrew word for peace (*Shalom*) retains.

Martin Luther King had a vision as personal and private as the sleeping child or the cross-legged meditator, but he turned it outward as a prayer for peace so that it became shared. President Sadat dealt in the politics of peace, which is usually paid for by other people's sacrifices. This time it was he who paid with his life.

Seraphic look

Jeremiah was scathing about those who cried "peace, peace when there was no peace". We should beware of those who use the word glibly about a state of mind which has no social dimension. By their fruits we shall know the peacemakers, not by the seraphic look on their faces.

The fragile jelly, peace, is coloured and watered down by that gooey substance—Love. Love which makes the world go round is no substitute for gelatine when it comes to holding together a lasting peace, for love is the most abused four letter word in the language.

The Greeks had four words for it. The first was affection of the kind that binds families together, or bosom pals. The second was the enthusiasm for something which can be—depending on the individual—a love of wisdom (philosophy), the English (anglophile), or postage stamps (philatelist). The third is sexual love and enough illustrative material is on show in cinemas for me not to need to labour this point. The fourth type of love is what the New Testament calls *agape* and it is this kind of love to which Jesus refers in calling on us to love our neighbour as ourself. It is caring love with a strong dash of mercy.

Permutations

Of course these categories do overlap. A married couple who are sexually compatible ought to score 3 out of 4, and if they share the same hobbies, it's a jackpot. So with four types of love and two kinds of peace, the phrase 'Peace and Love' can have a variety of meanings. Initially there are eight permutations—individual peace and love of collecting stamps makes Jack an introverted Boy, whereas social peace and erotic love makes what the Hippies meant by Peace and Love in the first place.

Why should the pairs and permutations stop there? The Social Peace and the idea of Family Love makes for an excellent political and moral principle. Add to it the idea of caring love and the potential permutations are endless. The mathematical equation should read: Peace multiplied by Love equals Infinity.

More serious mathematicians and religious persons will be interested to work out further equations: Peace, by the power of Love is God. God is equivalent to Love. War divided by Love is Peace. But I must stop, for I am turning Word into numbers not into flesh. For that is the equation of Peace and Love . . . one which we can all work out. □

An escape from the cycle of despair

"WHIT'S yer name hen?" the drunk and dishevelled man on the train asked the woman opposite him for the fourth time in a very loud voice. For the fourth time she replied that her name was Mary. "That wis my mother's name, Goad rest her soul," said the man for the fourth time and then had a flash of inspiration. "Ah telt ye that before," he recalled, his boozed eyes gazing emptily from side to side.

The faint waft of the regiment of unwashed drifted down the carriage as he carried on his harangue, vouchsafing the information that his wife had divorced him, not the other way round. It was a pathetic spectacle and to be honest I must confess to being more than a little annoyed at being trapped in a railway carriage and forced to listen to this poor soul lurching nearer to a grave in the gutter.

But it also stirred feelings of guilt and pity within me which I am still grappling to explain to myself. Forgive me if I share them with you, in the hope that they may echo your own sentiments.

Certainly this man could afford to travel by train. He had not reached the terminus *ad quem* down and outs go—and you can't get any further down than that. The thrashing rain has made the goal of the homeless—a warm and dry place to spend the night—that much more difficult to achieve.

Now that the long nights approach and the temperature is dropping towards the frosty lows of winter, their lot will become more miserable. Some will spend their giro cheque on a room in a lodging house. Some will frequent the hostels run by caring organisations which range from the most basic wooden bench with newspapers spread around. Others will go 'skippering' or sleeping rough in derelict buildings.

They come from many backgrounds, some from comfortable homes, and have found their various routes to inner and outer darkness.

It is no use telling a man who has received a thousand pounds a year in giro cheques that he has the means to better himself. Maintaining that sum of money (which 20 years ago was the threshold of affluence) is like trying to keep a snowball in your pocket by waiting until winter comes.

How many of us could keep our resolve and spirit after a few days without a bath, a week without a change of clothes. At first we would wince inwardly as eyes were averted from our faces when we opened conversation with another human being. Old friends would not want to know us, perhaps frightened that we would become a burden upon them.

Perhaps we would fling pride aside and ask someone for the price of a cup of tea, actually intending to spend it on that. We would be able to tell from their expressions that those from whom we begged did not believe us. As despair grew and self respect diminished we would take them at their unspoken word and go and buy a bottle of anaesthetic and uncork the genie who would play merry hell with the last vestige of hope of recovery.

No, not everyone goes that way. And those who do, usually do not only harm themselves. They often drag down members of their family into their coal cellar of degradation as they fuel the fires of self destruction.

Yet, flickering behind the twisted snarl of resentment of self and the world, is a flame of human spirit. How many of us have spent the time to get to know that person imprisoned in the vagrant? We pass by on the other side so easily. Yet I suspect that in society's down and outs we have the opportunity to learn a spiritual truth.

They can make us grateful that we have so much (there but for the grace of God go I . . .). They can act as a prick to our conscience to give time or money to help (we do unto the least of His brethren what we do unto Him). But above all they bring home the fragility of human power to rescue us from despair and the absence of hope.

Which one of us, by taking thought, can add a cubit to their stature, far less restore the lost cubits to the stature of one who has sunk so low.

Would that we could look straight into the eye of the destitute and kindle that low burning fire of self esteem into flame. But most of us would find that difficult. Only he who is with sin could do such a thing and not be playing God. Which brings us, logically, to God, the source of the grace necessary to escape the cycle of despair.

Which of us does not need that grace to give purpose to our lives, one we could not have by inventing meaning ourselves? The meaning comes from outside us. The grace to feel that the meaning and purpose rings true is from the same source. Thus it is meaningless to talk of bootstrap activities by which we or they who are less fortunate can lift themselves up.

The means of grace are therefore for all of us, deaf, dumb, or destitute. To deny them to the least of our brethren is to deny them to ourselves, for in saying they are irredeemable we are saying there is no hope for us either. It's a sobering thought and those who are not already drunk or on a train have a chance to do something about it—on the doorstep of their own city.   □

Closer to God with live broadcasting

THERE is an England where bees hum through warm English country gardens, where apple trees lean down low in Linden Lea, and where ladies in tweed skirts eat tea and crumpets in the afternoon. Through the French windows and across the lawn wafts the sound of choral evensong from a cathedral silhouetted against an autumn sky scattered with starlings who are startled into flight by the passage of a ploughman plodding his weary way homeward.

Ah yes, there is an England like that. But does it exist anywhere outside coiled up rolls of decaying celluloid of pre-war films? Do such images of England not lie buried with Rupert Brooke in some corner of a foreign field? The starlings have gone to nest in the hot-air ducts of a concrete and glass mountain in the city centre. The skyline is dominated not by spires, but pylons. The home-ward-bound ploughman roars his tractor across the flyover linking two fields bisected by the roar of the motorway beneath. The ladies watching the late afternoon episode of Crossroads are eating Mr Kipling cakes from their local Safeway, wearing their Crimplene trouser suits. *O tempora, o mores*!

There is, however, one exception to this vastly changed landscape. Choral evensong still wafts across the ether in the late afternoon, courtesy of BBC Radio 3. From 4 till 5 on Wednesdays and Fridays you can hear the sonorous tones of vicars reading the collect of the day and the distinctive sound of an Anglican choir.

Now, it is no secret that the audience for this programme is not large. Neither is the attendance at choral evensong in Anglican cathedrals up and down the land. Once upon a time a few years ago it was realised that the costs of circuits from the Post Office to broadcast choral evensong 'live' easily outstripped the courtesy fees paid to the participants. The perfectly reasonable suggestion was made that the service should be recorded. Not only would this save costs, but coughs and extraneous noises could be edited out. Awkward underruns when the organists had to fill with 10 minutes of organ voluntary at the end could be avoided. But the traditionalists would not have it. Worship, they said, must be live.

They seemed to be running against the tide of professionalism. Editing could make for better sound. Drama had been immeasurably improved by escaping the demands of live transmission when actors had to rush from one scene to the next. Music, both light and heavy, had been able to use new technology to improve the balance. Could the subtle sound of a choir not benefit from this?

At the time I thought so. The Scottish Roman Catholic bishops had insisted that Masses be broadcast live and held this demand long after other services were recorded for reasons of economy. Eventually, when Radio Clyde said "No recording, no Masses", and the bishops got themselves into a situation when it was one law for Clyde and another for the BBC, did the recorded Mass become a possibility. Years later I have come round to thinking that the proponents of live worship were right. It was a choral evensong from Southwark which convinced me.

The reasons are neither sentimental nor superstitious although I accept that arguments for live worship can fall sometimes into these categories. Sentimentality says that there will always be an England Church, and though you personally don't do anything about or believe in it, it's nice that someone does. That makes churches into museums. Worse still it is the superstition that the Holy Mass or a sermon or a prayer cannot be locked up on a roll of magnetic tape without being desecrated in some way. If that were so, any means of recording holy thoughts/words/deeds including scriptures would be suspect.

There are three reasons why live worship is better. The first is practical. Any broadcaster will tell you that there is something different and better about a live 'performance'. It takes more out of you and therefore you have more to give. The second reason is the immediacy of the moment. This goes without saying for the news and current affairs output, but it applies in the religious world also.

I listened to one choral song from Southwark Cathedral, prayers were said for a family whose names would mean nothing to the vast majority of listeners. It was the height of parochialism, but if churches are not parochial then who can be? It is of the essence of a religion which talks about hairs on your head being counted and not a sparrow falling from Heaven without mercy attending its descent, that it should be concerned about Mrs McSquirt's upcoming visit to hospital just as much as any public issue of 'importance'.

Recently the wife of a well-known Scottish public figure died. If you were to ask that man what is more important under Heaven—his public achievements or the death of that person—his answer would not be the majority one, the public one, but the private and particular one. Live broadcasting speaks to that particular, definite and identified target, you and me, and it does it now. The communication is not time-lapsed. It is not a circular slipped under your door to which you may or may not respond with a pre-paid envelope. The essence of preaching or prayer is that it asks for a response now, not later.

The third reason for supporting live worship is the very opposite. It is its generality. It is broad-cast. It includes all sorts of conditions of people in its audience, and it links them—in the cliche beloved by trade union spokesman—at that moment in time. It is perhaps dubious to argue that a prayer or worship becomes more efficacious if more people join in, but there is no doubt that man was created a social animal and ritual that

is shared is ritual that becomes more meaningful.

Choral evensong may not be the most popular pastime but it is a traditional and universal way of creating a linked worshipping community. Of course, there is such a community which appears rarely in public. It is that community of persons whose lives are dedicated to a life of prayer and contemplation. These monks and nuns do not do this for their own good. If you ask them they do it for OUR good.

Non-believers will see them as misguided optimists at best and fools at worse. But if you believe that there is a God then they are working for you in the sense that, for them, to pray is to work. If broadcast worship links us into that universal cycle of prayer and that reality, then it brings us closer to the presence of God. □

Fresh look at the 'great leveller'

IT is strange how hospitals smell differently when you have to visit them in a dire emergency. The distinctive odour seems to be concocted from institutional cleaning fluid and food (the two sometimes being similar) and mixed with disinfectant and the faint whiff of incontinence. At least that's the way it smells as the overheated air guffs each inhalation

89

into the lungs, producing a feeling of nausea. Perhaps it is because your stomach is already turning like a washing machine with tension that you feel that way.

The polished lino that you trod with ease visiting those friends who broke their legs on ski-ing holidays; the tarty blonde receptionist that you naughtily winked at as you went to visit the maternity ward; the unending corridors and the unfathomable numbering system of the wards which was a source of mild amusement.

Suddenly they are the dark stuff of which nightmare is made. You pad onward, the lino making a dull and unreal sound, the faces flit past uncomprehendingly as a soul in torment walks down the gloomy labyrinth.

Which is the dream and which is the reality? Is the hospital a nightmare, bathed in blue flashing light, the real picture, or is it the Christmas Eve scene in the children's ward by candlelight with Angels from the realms of which our fantasies about nurses are made? Possibly neither. But easy as it is to scoff away the sentimental picture of hospitals, the nightmare version still holds good for many patients and visitors.

It is easy for medical staff to forget this. To them it is a place of familiarity, the source of their authority whose vestments are a variety of uniforms from the consultant with white coat and stethescopic mitre, to the heavenly choir of angels coloured according to their status in the nursing hierarchy.

Dealing with relatives can be as trying as the clergyman finds the church attender who wants to give their testimony as they shake hands at the door. Sincere, and deeply felt as their feelings are, the professional does not always want to know. There is a place for professional detachment as long as it is dispensed with courtesy.

The surgeon, the ambulanceman, the undertaker, the minister, the lawyer sometimes have to face people whose close relatives are in a life-or-death predicament. Those patients or relatives will not be helped by the professional becoming emotionally involved. They want to rely on him to see them through. Besides we would question the competence of a suregon who was wiping tears from his eyes as he operated.

Compassion can be disciplined as can any other emotion. But I am not talking about emotion here. I am talking about what the Bible calls "bowels and mercies". The Greek word which underlines it might be more colloquially translated as 'gut feeling'.

This is not, however, a sermonette for professions, especially the medical one telling them to be nice to us, treat us as semi-intelligent and remember that it is our feelings that are involved as well as their reputations as physicians. (Nonetheless it is advice that would not go amiss.) This is not restricted to professionals for it applies wherever someone deals with the public.

Defences down

It ought to be directed also to blasé shop assistants, boorish taxi drivers or bitchy telephone operators. The difference is that the professional sees us when our defences are down. We can walk out of the shop, take back the tip or slam down the phone to expiate our fury at the former, but the professional deals with us in the raw, denuded of defence, not the fearsome British public but the fearful private grief-stricken relative.

Clusters of such people appear every day at the accident and emergency departments. A few find their way after a terrifying wait, up to the ward which receives the victims of road accidents.

In such a place I saw death come last week to an elderly man. I saw it on a television screen which protruded from the bed screens. The green blips flattened into a horrible horizontal line. Death, the great leveller, had come. But it was sent on its way by the skill of the nurse and soon the blips were back and the ventilator was puffing away.

It somehow was different from the way it is on the other kind of television screen. No drama, no glamour, only bowels and mercies which moved. The people are different too. The Prince who crashed his Ferrari lies next to the punk who fell off his motorbike. Bed is the great leveller.

"Bright eyes . . . burning with fire . . . how can you burn so brightly, then you burn so pale . . . Bright eyes." Outside in the sunshine through the tears I see the world with new eyes. The doors of perception are cleansed. A down and out is about to take a seat in the sun, one of the benches which have a plaque commemorating their donor. He peers at the plaque before he takes his seat, as if to know the name of his benefactor as he sits in the sun as the city traffic roars past. If he should stumble beneath the wheels of the juggernaut he will be taken to the ward I have left which, in its Victorian obsolescence, will have a plaque commemorating the benefactor of the bed.

At funerals we often sing the beautiful evening hymn 'The day Thou gavest Lord has ended'. The verse says, "The voice of prayer is never silent, Nor dies the strain of praise away". At the going down of the sun and in the morning we remember the dead of two world wars.

At teatime we announce in the news bulletins the names of those killed in the sectarian violence of Ulster, yet they have been vastly outnumbered in the past decade by those killed in road accidents in the same province.

Perhaps at the height of the sun and in the afternoon and amid the noise of the traffic, we should remember those whose eyes are dim and those who fight to help them see again. □

Thunder, lightning, valium

LIKE many people, I see the film of the book rather than read the book of the film. *Cloud Howe* is no exception. It is the middle book of Lewis Grassic Gibbon's trilogy which begins with *Sunset Song* and ends with *Grey Granite*.

The trilogy has been described as the best of Scottish novel writing in the twentieth century. I am not fit to judge the truth of that. But as a piece of religious writing, and as a study of the culture and character of rural life in Angus and Mearns, it is braw, affy braw.

If you enjoyed the BBC version, as I have, then you will remember the Revd Robert Colquohoun preaching his apocalyptic sermon on the text, "Lord remember me when Thou comest into Thy Kingdom!"

"This year when hunger and want filled the land the counsellors of the nation told for our guidance that more hunger and poverty yet must come . . . there is no hope for the world at all— except it forget the dream of the Christ, forget the creeds that are forged in His shadow when their primal faith in the God was loosed, and turn and seek with unclouded eyes, not that sad vision that leaves hunger unfed, the wail of children in the unending dark, the cry of human flesh eaten by beasts . . . but a stark sure creed that will cut like a knife through the doubt and disease— men with unclouded eyes may yet find it. . . ."

It all reads rather less dramatic when it is plucked out from the novel into this column, but it rings so true when you have opened the pages and slipped into the imaginative world of Segget village, or had it recreated for you by television.

But the book and the film ring true for me not because they were well done, but because I lived in Segget. As the characters unfold I shriek with recognition as another incident triggers off recognition of my days in Segget. Of course, it was not called that, but there was a village provost every bit as much a bully as Provost Hogg. There was a hard-man farmer, there was the posh laird who belonged to a different class and different era— and there were council houses whose folk got the rough end of the harvest before anyone else. If I had stayed in Segget I might have become a Socialist like Mr Colquohoun.

It is often thought our history consisted of a rural Scotland in which there was a school in every parish and in which every Saturday night numerous cottars brought out their Bibles and began to read the Scriptures. This is illusion. The real picture was a hard rural life with the majority of people living in harsh poverty and having very little to do with religion. Even in the boom times of the Victorian era, the bulk of the working classes had nothing to do with the Church. The minister was a figure of influence but very often thought to be the laird's man, for the landowner appointed him in the period 1712-1874. But he was not a feckless chiel and spoke back with the same muscular message that the ploughmen would not shrink from giving him.

We have lost all that as a nation. Ministers are supposed to be nice people, not red-blooded with passion in their veins. Ploughmen don't bother them much now.

In the closing chapter of *Sunset Song* there is a passage that reminds me of the coda of Gotterdammerung when the Rhine overflows its banks and sweeps away that world of the gods into oblivion. The minister has gone to the hill above Kinraddie to deliver the epitaph for the dead of the Great War, among whom was Chris's husband. She then married the Revd Robert Colquohoun whose words on this occasion contrast sharply with the flashing sword of the apocalypse which comes down like lightning at the end of *Cloud Howe*. This is more like a plough which gently turns over the earth in which memories are buried.

"With them we may say there died a thing older than themselves, these were the last of the peasants, the last of the Old Scots Folk. A new generation comes up that will not know them except as a memory in a song, they passed with the things that seemed good to them with loves and desires that grow dim and alien in the days to be. It was the old Scotland that perished then and we may believe that never again will the old speech and the old songs, the old curses and the old benedictions rise but with alien effort to our lips."

Colquohoun's two sermons are the two faces of Scotland. Thunder and lightning. Peace and the sword. The doppelganger which stalks our village

of Brigadoon is the shadow cast by the City of God, its reflection in the river Styx. Whether we regret the passing of such places or rejoice in it, they are still with us, with their confusing mixture of kindness and cruelty. They are the bricks and mortar of society which we rebuild in every new age. We have new forms of enslavement. The cottar had cheap whisky to help him forget. Now we have valium. Where Calvinism was once the opium of the peoples, now valium is the valium of the peoples.

Lest all seem to be setting sun and cloud shadows, perhaps we should be encouraged by the idealistic words with which Colquohoun ended his *Sunset Song* before the evil of Segget engulfed him. "Let us believe that the new oppressions and foolish greeds are no more than mists that pass." □

Those for whom the bells really toll

IT used to be called the Great War, now it is the First World War. The former reeked of chauvinism and the glorification of war; the latter carried the ominous implication that it was the first in a series of world wars. The ridiculous title of the 'War to end Wars' is now never used except in mocking irony. Perhaps the factual 1914-18 War enables us to remember it better.

But remember is exactly what some would rather not do. They believe that the survivors should bury their dead and the rest of us should try to forget this blood stain on the reputation of Western civilisation. Attention is diverted forward in time by claiming that the Armistice only planted the seeds through which the Nazis rose to power.

Such critics look with pitying scorn upon the white-haired colonels who stand stiffly to attention for two whole minutes in the stark November air at a village war memorial on which is carved the names of men who are scarce remembered by their own descendants, never mind by the rest of the village. Then comes the church parade at which the uniformed youth stand gawkily and uncomprehending, knowing nothing of the mud and the mustard gas, knowing neither glaur nor glory.

This, many would say, is the state of affairs, and thus they would reason, it is time we forgot to remember. "Let us now praise famous men," says the reading so often chosen for Remembrance Sunday, but it is now the day of the anti-hero or the amoral man whose organisation is his justification. It is the day of CI5 and 007. No names, no pack drill—only rank and number.

Kitchener might be the inventor of a kind of room or Haig the distiller of a brand of whisky, for all the passion that they arouse in the modern breast. At the eleventh hour of the eleventh day, the traffic will merely rumble by the war memorials which will have had their share of Sunday observance.

A landmark

As a person born after the Second World War, I might be supposed to share this attitude, but I do not. The war of 1914 is to me a landmark in the history of civilisation that we ignore at our peril. It was a war of the people, not of professional soldiers. It was fought with patriotic fervour, but it was poets who brought back the true dispatches which spoke of the nobility of man who had once again experienced the Fall and was stuck in the mud of a trench in Flanders.

As Lewis Grassic Gibbon describes them in *Sunset Song*, they were the last of the old Scots folk. Every one of their families had lost at least one member. Never again would an army go to war expecting that it would be a professional affair never involving the whole of a population. War was now something which spread like an ocean until two thirds of the world was covered in the wake of the tears.

"At the going down of the sun and in the morning, we shall remember them." So easily we can fall into thinking of Remembrance Day as an affair of the armed forces and of the veterans. There they all are by the Cenotaph, laying wreaths in waves which break, break, break on the cold white stone and stain it with red. Each poppy a heart that was broken in mourning the departed.

Some memories never seem to fail. As a wave breaks on the shore and another takes its place, so the Chelsea pensioners seem to be sempiternally young, reclothing a new generation in their distinctive uniforms.

But death is not the prerogative of the soldier. As the poppy is the symbol of remembrance, so also are the fallen leaves of autumn the symbol of the frailty of human life and its inevitable fate. Why therefore cannot the dead of the two last wars be our inspiration to face up to the horror of death? There is a time for laughter and a time for tears. Surely autumn is the time for tears and the chance to be mellow of soul and think on those who have departed this life. *L'Allegro* is meaningless without *Il Penseroso*. Those who do not face up to their own mortality are supremely to be pitied for they probably re-live a second childhood crying in the dark for a light.

Whether we are Right-wing or Left-wing, patriot or pacifist, Christian or atheist, German or British, we are all a part of the continent. If a clod be washed from the continent, said John Donne, then it is by that much the less. So when the church bell tolls on Remembrance Sunday, it is tolling for the dead of the wars, it is tolling for mankind past and present, it is tolling for our nearest and dearest— and for us.

Electric shock

If you are a believer, you will have faith in the life to come. If you are an agnostic you will hope. But all of us fear. There is therefore scope for courage, not only in battle but in life, affirming life against death. There is much to be said for the melancholy practices of our forebears who forced people to view the dead, so that their electric shock of grief might be earthed along with the coffin. Yet we conspire to make it the great obscen-

ity, the word that has one more than four letters and mentioned less frequently.

Perhaps I have eaten the seeds of a poppy that is grown farther east than Flanders, but I have a dream. It is that people will look at the trenches of Flanders as they were, with the corpses and the mud and the rats. All the poetry of our nation cannot wash the stench from out of our nostrils, so that we might know what war was and then, in reflecting, realise that it all will be as flowers compared to what a nuclear strike would mean.

Yet more recently a man called Haig said that one nuclear weapon could be launched if war broke out in Europe. He is a general, not an intoxicating liquor. I wonder if history is going to repeat itself. With one difference. This *will* be the war to end wars . . . □

The fateful day God went on trial at Dachau

THERE are times which come to all of us when Fate seems to be against us. On the trivial level it is the rainy day when the car won't start and we miss the bus and stand at the bus stop to be splashed by a passing car. It is when the power cut coincides with the cliff-hanging episode of our favourite soap opera.

Worse still is the situation which

we cannot control. The traffic jam in which we are caught travelling to an important appointment. The phone box which has been vandalised and from which an urgent call is required. All the will in the world, or competence or worry for that matter, does not exempt us from these events which place us in the hands of Fate.

Applying reason does not help, for power cuts or buses (notwithstanding that literature of fiction known as timetables) are random. They reinforce the fact that we live in a world of chance. Certainly, someone decides to pull the lever for the power cut and there may be a reason behind it (spreading the load evenly between areas) but its effect upon us—unless we have advance warning—is essentially chance.

To accept that principle is to be able to apply reason to the situation. It is within the bounds of probability that we would arrive at the bus stop just after the bus. It will also be reasonable to expect that another bus will be along in a minute. But that is as far as reason goes. To try to apply reason further to the situation, for instance in asking, "why did Fate dictate that I would miss the bus?" or to extend it further by saying, "why did God allow this to happen to me?" is not reasonable. It does not solve the problem either by introducing an imputed reason, e.g. God must have meant me to be late, to teach me something.

The territory which lies beyond reason is the land of meaning. It is a long, flat land through which we journey in darkness, lit only by the small circle of our own lamp of faith. Occasionally a traveller who has seen the mountaintop (and whom we have no reason to disbelieve) encourages us on our way by describing pastureland which lies ahead. We accept the promise of this land.

But to all of us there come experiences, flickering insights in the shadows beyond our lamp of faith. We see the tortured faces of the suffering millions, whether dying of hunger or persecution, whether dying the lingering death from toxic chemicals in a factory accident or the quick deliberate death that has come to the decomposing body on the tarmac from a hijacker's bullet.

Closer to home are the loved ones over whom death has cast its shadow. The hollow hope that in our lives we will escape personal suffering, bereavement, betrayal, malice and injustice, is for most of us only a hope.

Perhaps worst of all is the suffering which is deliberately inflicted, person to person. Cruelty whether in the kitchen, the classroom or the concentration camp is a way of injecting an evil logic into the darkness of meaninglessness. I am suffering so you will suffer too.

The paradigm of ultimate suffering in our age must be the concentration camp, and there is a Rabbinical story of how the Jews at Dachau decided one day to put God on trial. Why had He allowed this to happen to His chosen people? How could He be anything but a monster to allow the innocent to go daily to death in the gas chambers? The jury found God guilty of the crimes against humanity. Whereupon a Rabbi reminded them, after they had pronounced the verdict: "Gentlemen it is the sabbath. We must needs attend to our prayers." And they trooped off to do just that.

The story would be sick if it did not touch a nerve deep in the human psyche. It is natural for us to doubt and even to resent God. To demand the justice we have earned and to escape the injustice we do not deserve. But deep down we know that such reason does not apply in the vale of tears. So we attend to our prayers. That may seem a mockery to those who see life as idiotic, full of sound and fury and signifying nothing.

To them I would say three things. The first is that deeply felt experiences of joy or pain should be faced as insights into reality. None is ever wasted. To have travelled into the desert is to have gone somewhere. The second is to look back at pleasures gained and problems seen through. These are progress.

But the darkness will still abound if the third perspective is not envisaged. This is to keep travelling. To attend to the direction in which we ought to go. To stand and assess progress is to stand still spiritually. It is the peace of the graveyard, not of the fast flowing river.

Often we wait for Godot to come to us. To meet us halfway. Perhaps that is why our dark world still clings to Christmas as to no other festival of the Christian year. But those who do not travel toward the darkness and towards the star, will find like the tramps of Beckett's parable that those who wait for Godot to come to them, will wait in vain. □

The worst kind of have-not

IS it coincidence that features and appeals for children in need have been tumbling out just in time for Christmas? If you think that is a cynical thought, it is not. For the whole problem of child vulnerability was given a horrific topicality by the trial of the child molester who had finally murdered in his frustrated attempts to satisfy his sickening appetite on a young girl. The forlorn pile of Christmas presents at the foot of her family tree that will now never be opened is, like the cairn of stones that covered her mutilated body, a reminder that evil and depravity still stalk the world, claiming even the most innocent as victims.

That is hardly new. Nor is the need at Christmas to remember the children. Who does not feel a lump in the throat when the little angels trot out to the front of the church or school and pipe Away in a Manger with dewy eyes and beguiling innocence? To let a tear trickle down at that sight is not sentimental. It is letting Christmas reach the parts of our emotions that other seasons of the year do not reach.

That warm and reassuring tradition is our candle against the dark and the cold world. We can cope with its contradiction. Bleakness and loneliness outside. Shelter and warmth at the Inn. Cruelty overcome by tender love such as the bond which protects the new-born baby in its mother's arms. But can we cope with the other contradiction which has grown alongside traditional Christmas, the contradiction between have and have-not?

Nor am I talking about the contradiction between those who have a job and those who do not. This is truly tragic, and after the numbing years of realisation that the slag heap of unemployment statistics was not going to disappear from the landscape, nor was the harsh complacency which advocated it as a kind of medicine for ailing industry, it would appear that even the Government's best supporters are anxious that something be done. Would that it can, and at least thinking about the problem is to be aware of those in need.

Another tragic have/have-not divide in the world is between those who have food to eat at Christmas and those who do not. Ethiopia lies like a gaunt shadow across the landscape of 1984. Even if a tiny fraction of those who heard the famous Band Aid record gave a thought to the plight of the hungry millions, it was a success.

But taking thought for the unemployed or the hungry does not employ or feed them, even if it does add a cubit to our self-esteem. There is a sense in which we seem to be spitting across the wind in trying to combat these huge gulfs between haves and have-nots. There is another, even greater, contradiction which seems insuperable. It is far more pervasive than poverty, more destructive of the human being even than hunger. It is the absence of love.

This is the greatest have/have-not gap of our times. The contradiction is that we now have a globe that has been shrunk by electronic communications and we do not know our neighbours. We have toys for children which can bring Star Wars into the living room and we have weapons controlled from the skies above us which can destroy cities. There is a tragic innocence about today's child playing happily with his Darth Vadar spaceship. To him it is a toy. He does not know that even now the capacity to destroy the entire globe exists many times over and resides in the hands of a few.

Peace is fragile, but never before have the consequences of it being broken been so terrible. Love is difficult, but never before has there been as much hate broadcast throughout the world. If we ever needed Christmas, we need it now.

Even the children, those eternal springs of new hope and life, are being corrupted earlier. Schoolroom anarchy as never before. Drug-taking to escape reality. It is a miserable picture. You don't recognise it? Good. It means you are part of the solution already. There is nothing I would like better than to be proved wrong in this doom and gloom assessment. But the paucity of peace and goodwill at large forces me to one of two conclusions. Either we are dependent on mankind to work itself out of the mess (in which case I believe we are doomed), or there is a higher force/consciousness whom many call God which can reach out to us and transform us.

Two thousand years ago such a process started at the milestone of the heavens marked by the era of Pisces. The Age of the Fish started with fishermen who left their nets and began a revolution upon which the grandeur of Western civilisation was built. It surely does not matter whether it started in a stable or by a lakeside. The change of direction, the impulse to create a new world founded on compassion, was there.

When you look at any baby it is there. And for all our test-tube capabilities with embryos we still are confronted with the mystery of how those cells and double helices multiply to form a mature, loving, breathing human being. Even if we look at the heavens this Christmas and think that God has abandoned us, drawing the era of the Fishermen to a close, then we should use a different scale. Take the microscope out and find that mystery still lies at the heart of life itself. See it grow into a baby. But from then on through life, love, or the lack of it, takes over. That's the bit that's up to us. May you experience peace and goodwill this Christmas.   □

Hungry eyes that reflect our own guilt

THERE was a time when having a Christian conscience meant feeling guilty about the starving millions. Even those who did not share the more orthodox believer's subscription to the creeds and dogmas of the institutional churches, could at the very least share in caring ministry by reaching into their pockets when Christian Aid week came around. A starving mouth does not recite creeds. It first and foremost needs to be fed.

That was the aim of the big charities like Oxfam or Christian Aid. For those who wanted a drop of doctrine to sweeten the spoon, or at least be sure that the hand wielding it held the same doctrinal position as themselves, there were similar charities such as SCIAF (the Scottish Catholic International Aid Fund) or TEAR Fund which draws its support from evangelicals such as Cliff Richard, who did tremendous work for the starving people of Bangladesh.

It all conformed to the scriptural injunction to feed the hungry, clothe the naked and shelter the homeless. It was particularly popular in the heady days of the 'sixties' when youth groups sang "When I needed a neighbour were you there?" and played guitars in church, and schoolchildren were taught the parable of the Good Samaritan over and over again in their R.E classes. Martin Luther King's 'dream' speech on the brotherhood of man was shown over and over again on television.

Cynical

Now it has all changed. We have seen the horrors of Vietnam. We have grown more cynical. We have seen the shadow of the mushroom cloud come nearer. And, meanwhile, most of us forgot about the starving millions.

Of course, the flow of money to these charities has not dried up. But it has become more of a habit than a duty. We have begun to doubt the international socialist impulse to send Government funds to Third World countries. The post of Minister of Overseas Development exists no longer. With over 3,000,000 unemployed it is easy to believe that charity begins at home.

Perhaps we have become tired or bored by the seemingly thankless task of irrigating the vast desert of the hungry whose heads are as countless as the grains of sand. The social gospel has gone into a second phase which is not so appealing as the first. The agnostics who were happy to clap their hands and sing in the 'sixties alongside their Christian brothers now feel perhaps that they do not need a religious setting.

The moral-social dimension has become the social-political dimension and there is less need for religion. Or so one might think from the outside.

There have been churchmen who are anxious to prove their relevance to this new situation. Some of them feel that the way to do so is through civil disobedience. That way they will break into the stockade of indifference and cynicism.

But I do not want to write about that. I do not want to go that way. I do not want to start fighting before the battle has begun. Because once we are set on that road we will even more be turned in upon ourselves in a civil war of moral and social differences. It is tempting to be distracted by that theme this week when the British Council of Churches has sounded a trumpet call to the militant social conscience. To ignore it is not political prejudice or a desire to return to the days of those dreams and a time when the liberal conscience was not soiled by its inability to live up to its ideal.

Doomed to die

It is not an ideal that turns me aside, but a picture of a tiny starving child aged two years and weighing less than 10lb. He was one of the thousands who are doomed to die in Ethiopia this week. Not next week, but *this* week. His little swollen tummy cannot wait until Christian Aid week comes around. By then he will have joined those other tiny little bundles wrapped in rags and lowered into the hastily scooped out holes in which the refugees of the Ethiopian drought return to the dust.

Perhaps it is a sign of hope that 'News at Ten' considered this to be the lead item on Monday. The shocking facts of the situation were powerfully brought home by the film report. Pictures speak louder than words and no matter what I write here or how many casualty statistics I quote, I cannot possibly convey the haunting pity of these wide eyes staring at the camera, waiting to be helped.

It is an appeal that I cannot deny— and because actions speak louder than pictures or words, I feel that I must send my fee for this article to Christian Aid. It is the very least I can do, otherwise my sympathy is oil for anointing the dead, my concern is the reflection of my own guilt in their eyes rather than a true impulse to help them. If you share that impulse the address is: Christian Aid, George IV Bridge, Edinburgh.

Why I know that I must do this is

that I must respond while my ability lasts to weep at 'News at Ten'. Tears can so easily turn to drought and despair to cynicism. Already I feel anger alongside the sadness that the United States of America will not be sending any aid because of the Communist nature of the military rulers in Ethiopia.

When the politics of a person's country is enough to prevent them receiving life-saving sustenance then a terrible new factor has entered into our international climate. It is spiritual drought—and close behind it will come sickness and famine, and who can say that is not a judgment that we are bringing upon ourselves. □

A glimpse of life in all its fullness

Easter
THERE is always someone worse off than yourself. Perhaps that is a cliche but cliches usually become such because they are well-worn repetitions of good common sense. They can be rendered as poetry and attain the status of proverbs, or they can be couthy sayings heard at grandmother's knee, but they are true nevertheless.

Of course, when it comes to assessing how badly off we really are, there is a tendency for our egocentricity to come to the fore. No one could possibly be as badly hurt as we are. No one cares as much, is as sensitive, so well motivated, so misunderstood, has so much to give. Blah-blah-blah.

In short, our image of ourselves is very rarely the one that the outsider sees. Most of us would like to think that the truth, if humility and honesty bids us recognise, is not necessarily our version, lies somewhere between the two pictures. But there is still someone worse off than we are.

It is easier to spot the ones who are materially worse off. They are starving. Or they are walking the streets in threadbare garments. At the very basic level of filling their stomach with food they are at the bottom of the pile. Then there are those with inadequate housing or no job. There are the chronically ill, the terminally ill, the handicapped, the senile, the insane. On and on the list goes. Each a label, but each a real condition under which a human being lives. It is pretty miserable and it is the truth.

Then there are those who have what they need in material terms but lack love or respect. The lonely, the depressed, the nervy, the guilt-ridden.

There is a third category of sufferer. It contains those who are comfortably off in material terms and who do not suffer from any of the traumas of the second category. Here we find the brash, the successful, the creepy crawlers who get to the top any way they can, the smug, the self-loving, the swinger, the chancer, the over-indulger and the couldn't-care-less sophisticate. Yes, the very people who seem to have made it to the top of the heap, without falling victim to either of the other categories of pain.

In short it is a description of

101

someone that many people envy—and given half a chance would become right away. It is a picture of a great many people—seen from the outsider's point of view of course.

But these people suffer one handicap. The ability to hand out pain and to take anything else they can get their hands on. Handicap? Yes, handicap because they are incapable of experiencing life in any depth. That is why, when their upward spiral bends back on itself they crash spectacularly, flat on their backs. They do not feel, so they have to develop anaesthetics for reality. Drink, drugs, porn.

In case you are wondering what this has to do with Easter, I believe it has a great deal. The people who crucified Jesus belonged to the third category. His pain belonged to the first two categories—physical privation and mental agony. But because of his capacity to show a love beyond anything our self-centred natures can muster, his pain was beyond anything we can understand.

Certainly there have been innocent political prisoners more cruelly tortured. But imagine a person who has given his love and his loyalty to his friends, who is then abandoned by them in his moment of need. Imagine then loving both these friends and the persecutors and refusing to be beaten into hate. No, I do not think I can imagine it. Can you?

I try to imagine it as I gaze upon the cross of Calvary and through its pain, its mystery and its triumph over hate I can see a glimmer of what life might be in all its fullness. Not a life without pain or difficulty, nor of unending joyous life, but a life enriched by being caught up into a deeper reality, one that is obscured from someone who can think only in selfish terms of their own pain, and completely hidden from someone who has made their animal appetite dominant so that only physical pain, not existential pain, is ever felt.

The cross is a paradox, a symbol of degradation turned into a triumphant message. It is not easily or glibly understood, but when we survey the 'wondrous cross' it reminds us that there is no one good enough but God to have done that, and no matter how humble or gentle and loving we manage to be there will always be someone better than ourselves, who was truly the Son of God.   □

The special day for cards that say it all

EVERYONE has a mother. So the potential customers for Mother's Day gifts, cards and flowers represent a large slice of humanity. Even when babes in arms and those whose mother has long ago passed on, are excluded, mothers and sons and daughters are a sizable section of the population of this country.

There are of course some who object to Mother's Day as blatant commercialism. They say it is cashing in on Mothering Sunday which exists to celebrate a wider event, and that Mother's Day has become a secular equivalent. I cannot agree with this at all. For a start there is the exhortation of the Fifth Commandment, "Honour your father and mother." If it takes a special day to remind some people of this obligation then so be it. If someone has the entrepreneurial wit to print cards which say it for us then should we complain? Is this not better than not saying it at all?

For others who prefer to say it with flowers, nature obliges by opening her ample bosom of lily complexion, and for those who cannot afford the humble daffodil there is the modest crocus or snowdrop. In other words, there is no excuse—except for those who do not enjoy the kind of relationship with their mother that could be described as loving or harmonious.

Prodigal sons and daughters. Bitter matriarchs. These are sadly not the prerogative of soap operas but all too common in life. Their consequences are families torn by strife or separated by enmity. A peek behind the curtains is to encounter the soap opera which has become kitchen sink drama, the Freudian nightmare rendered as Greek tragedy. There is a hollow ring to Mother's Day in such homes.

But even if there is little love to be celebrated for those families, is there not some honour which can be salvaged from the situation. "Honour thy father and mother" says the Commandment. Honour is not necessarily love, but respect is surely part of it. The Commandment, however, goes on, "That your days may be long in the land that the Lord has given you".

At first that sounds like base self interest. A bargain struck so that one may be looked after in one's old age. But any emotional transaction can be reduced by cynicism to such self-interested dimensions. A more generous view would say that the parent who gave life to their offspring is not owed anything in law, but part of the value of that life is in being able to show generosity and respect towards others rather than dealing with them on the basis of what we get out of it all the time.

It is this quality which distinguishes the ethical content of religious systems from a set of rules made to keep society stable. The Ten Commandments can be viewed like a set of rules to keep the vagabond Israelites on the straight and narrow. But that was only part of their purpose. The social section about stealing, adultery and covetousness comes at the end. Prime place is given to honour and adoration of the Creator God, the giver of life. Right in the middle, linking the two sections, is the Fifth Commandment which is not simply a social command but an injunction to see the parent child relationship as part of that divine life-creating process.

Where created life is not honoured it is not only the aborted foetuses which perish but a whole generation which has grown old without accumulating that respect and honour from its offspring. The generation which fought the Second World War has now grown old and its offspring, the babies of the Welfare State, now face this question. Life expectancy has risen, but people's expectations of one another have fallen. The old have become a problem. 'Pensioned off' is a phrase which rings with the lack of respect which our society has for its senior citizens.

As the numbers of pensioners rise inexorably in the years to come, our society will face an acute test of its respect for the fathers and mothers of the post war era. Will we see them as a problem or an asset? Will we honour them or institutionalise them?

With honour goes the notion of nobility and to me the noblest people tomorrow on Mother's Day will be those who go with a heavy heart to visit their mother in a mental hospital or geriatric ward. Senility seems to negate the nobility of human life. Yet love and respect for their father and mother have not died in these people.

Much as one wishes that irreversible senility will swiftly dissolve into easeful death, those who have a loved one in this position go on honouring, loving, visiting and sustaining what is left of the image of the mother or father they knew. By so doing they illuminate the truth which all mothers recognise as they give birth—that in human life we come closest to comprehending the divine, the image of God. When the darkness of sorrow descends, sometimes we have difficulty in comprehending that truth. But it is not the shadow of the person which occupies the geriatric ward that we honour, but the light which once lit them from within.

The world will be a darker place if we do not seize the chance to grasp that torch to hand a new generation.

If Saints' Days are for celebrating heroines of the faith, Mother's Day is the Saints' Day in reverse, when we get a chance to show a little valour and honour ourselves. □

A Good Friday hymn for our anxious times

IN the now demolished Overgate in Dundee there was a drug store on the American model. It opened on Sundays and sold all kinds of exotic drinks (non-alcoholic) which were made from various brightly coloured syrups to which hot water was added. The aroma of these wafted out to me as I passed when a small boy and I longed to taste these esoteric brews of bright green and red and purple. The latter was probably blackcurrent but what the others were I cannot tell, for the shop has long since disappeared. Along the front of the shop window was written the name of the owners in bold letters—Greenhill.

Ludicrous it may be, but perhaps understandable to those who know the power of thought association in young minds, I still cannot get that shop out of my mind when I sing a certain hymn. As you have probably already guessed, the hymn in question begins: "There is a green hill far away. ...." But that slightly absurd way of looking at Good Friday is where I began as a child and as such it still has a bearing on where my pilgrimage of faith will end.

No matter that Calvary was probably not a green hill and more likely and symbolically a skull-shaped rock called Golgotha. The image of the green hill is still what comes first to many adults who were not exposed to my exotic drugstore, when they think of the crucifixion. They have probably added a daffodil or two in their mind's eye, because they probably grew up in a church bedecked with daffodils at Easter, sang happily of how sweet the lily grows beneath Siloam's shady rill at every baptism they attended, and had the image of the daffodil of Wordsworth flashed upon the inward eye which is the bliss of school-itude.

Other than Christmas, no other part of our faith is so coloured by childhood images and impressions than Easter. The picture we have of Good Friday is particularly susceptible to this because it is here that we encounter an enigma that we struggle to understand through images. The King who was crucified; the suffering servant who rules; the man who by dying lives eternally. Blood that is red like the wine of communion. A gallows, which was the Roman symbol of criminals' execution, becomes the sign of triumph used by the followers of Jesus the Jew who were themselves Gentiles. Yes, only pictures can put over a story like that.

But when we come to reflect on the meaning of it all, here too words begin to fail. That hymn I spoke of goes on: "He died that we might be forgiven, he died to make us good, he died that we might go at last to heaven, saved by His precious blood." This is a very crude way of stating the doctrine of substitutionary atonement and one that I do not find very convincing.

Lest this be thought to be some intellectual snobbism acquired at university, I must say that I have found the verse dissatisfying since the age of 10 and said so to the Sunday School superintendent who was not able to convince me either. I thoroughly sympathise with those who struggle over this difficult concept.

Having declared my childhood prejudices, let me now say that I believe the picture we are offered of Good Friday often resembles the exotic concoctions of Messrs Greenhill. The royal purple of blackcurrant is the view of those who emphasise the kingly ransom that was paid by Jesus on our behalf. The red of blood is the colour seen by those who emphasise the suffering endured by Jesus on the Cross. The green pastoral shade is the landscape of those who see Calvary as a haunting note on the cello, a symphony of unrequited love for mankind whose poignancy ends on a triumphant note.

The true picture lies in a subtle blend of the colours. The resulting potion would be quite unpalatable and indigestible, which may explain why so many traditions within the Christian Church concentrate on one type at the expense of the others. The Catholic crucifix shows a figure twisted in suffering, in the Protestant cross the figure is gone, departed to a higher, triumphant place. By emphasising or alternately ignoring the suffering or the triumph, we make the paradox lopsided and the picture hangs squint.

Many of us are poised somewhere between Good Friday and Easter morning in our world today and in our view of Easter. The oppression which is so manifest in many countries mirrors the brute imperial force which dominated Palestine in the time of Jesus. There are the freedom fighters, the guerrillas, the prisoners of conscience and of expediency. The jails are full and the bellies are empty. Isaiah's vision of the Prince of Peace who would herald a day when ploughshares would come from swords, is all too unreal for those who live in the countries in which war is still raging.

But that is the backdrop of today's Calvary. The characters are still discernible as human beings with tears in their eyes. At the centre of events is the figure of Christ crucified. But today the hill is inverted—it is the abyss of darkness. Surrounding it, staring into it for meaning, are the faithful followers waiting for the dark night to pass into dawn.

For some the wait is a whole lifetime. Think of the spinsters who two generations ago waited for the return of a young man from Flanders. He did not return. No one rose to take his place, so their life was changed. Not thwarted, but changed. There are the other elderly people who have worked for an end that never came. The cross they contemplate is the one that negates and crosses out what they have achieved. It no longer seems to be important or having been worth the effort. There are the old for whom the cross means rejection by those they have loved. Love has not brought its reward and the price of having cared is to suffer.

For them (the unconverted who stand at the dateline of Good Friday) it is facile for the preacher to say that what has happened has been done for them, so cheer up and let us rejoice. The preacher who focuses on the cross is to them like a corpse at a wake. But, says St Paul, what have we to preach but Christ crucified? So we must then ask if the Christian message is doomed to remain one of consolation for those who wait for belief.

Two things bring me beyond that point. Neither can be described as an argument which proves the case of a theological system. The first is that somehow the inadequate arguments for the atonement become better when they are sung. The Easter hymn is better than the Easter sermon. Like people in peril on the sea whose ocean liner of safe civilised comfort has gone down, we have taken to the lifeboats. By singing the old hymns, even the saddest ones—'Abide with me,' 'When I survey the wondrous cross,' 'O sacred head sore wounded'—such a dispirited band can recover an intangible hope that is not contained in the words but generated by singing the tunes. Singing is good for the soul. Even if it is not a means of salvation, singing, "I know that my redeemer liveth" can help us to *know* rather than require us to have belief before we open our mouths. Ask the agnostics who have glimpsed the magic of Christmas by singing words they found strange.

The second Easter crutch for my belief is to look at what the other religious systems have to offer in answer to the problem of suffering. If it is the will of Allah, then Allah is not good but cruel. If it is the karma which says that we must go round again being miserable until we get it right, then it denies what I feel to be true about the infinite mercy and love of God. The other gods ride to their thrones; but Jesus stumbles. Not a god has wounds but He alone. To our wounds—psychological and physical—past and present—these wounds speak. They say what generations of preachers have taken as the text for their good news. "God so loved the world that he gave his only begotten Son that whosoever believed in Him should not perish but have everlasting life." □

Reality through religion

GOD rules the world from a position approximately north-north west of Craigiebarn Road in Dundee. He does so from a computer bank controlled by levers, and He is male and has a white beard.

This picture of God, which I held as a child, reflected the view I had of the world. Bordered by the trees and the cul-de-sac to the north, my view was southward and I assumed that the Deity would share this perspective. Interested as I was in science, I assumed that only the most modern equipment would suffice to control the affairs of the world, and since the mighty micro had not yet been invented, God had to make do with the technology available to us all in the early fifties.

Ironically, right beneath that position above the clouds in Craigiebarn Road there now reposes a Royal Observer Corps post and a nuclear fallout shelter beneath which defences can be organised in the event of a nuclear attack.

I have now come to believe that it will not be God who will pull the lever but some cog in the machinery built to defend us from one another. But no doubt he will do it in the name of God. . . .

The tendency to project our human view of the world onto the Deity is called anthropomorphism. We see God through rosy, flesh-coloured spectacles. We expect Him to act in accordance with our 'higher nature.' We use our reason to figure out *why* God did something, and we give him the benefit of the doubt when we come across difficult problems such as why He chose to give someone breast cancer. For a God who controls (even with levers) is in charge, responsible and ultimately guilty of such acts.

That was my view in teenage years when rationality was encouraged and logic led me to reject such a God.

It was only in my early twenties that I grasped a different view of God. It was on a sunny Sunday afternoon in my room at St Salvator's Hall in St Andrews. Time stood still.

The trees were framed against the western sky. A sense of peace pervaded the room. Whichever direction I chose would be the correct one.

Since then I have encountered a description in T. S. Eliot's quotation from the thirteenth century mystic Juliana of Norwich—"All shall be well, And all manner of thing shall be well". Yes, I think it was a mystical experience. Goodness and peace suffused everything, but not like a manic 'high' which I knew would pass. This feeling would pass, but while it lasted I felt that I was experiencing reality which is normally hidden from perception. So strong was this conviction that I was prepared to act on the strength of it and commit myself to believe, because of the momentum which it gave me. Over twenty years have not diminished that conviction, but that does not make the testimony any more valid for an outsider.

That is the trouble with mystical experiences. They are essentially personal and private. The testimony of two witnesses is not possible. Further, such experiences are very difficult to put into words as the large collection of woolly and pious literature of mysticism testifies.

Re-reading my account of my own episode I see it to be hopelessly inadequate. Yet I believe that mystics have a grasp of the *real* world, not the one we see most of the time. The mystic is *not* akin to the drunk man, or the hallucinating drug addict, or the vitamin-starved fasting nun, or the hypnotised girl in the stage hypnotism show. What the mystic experiences is *not* an overlay of reality or a distortion of it, as in the above cases, but a situation in which (in Blake's words) "the doors of perception are cleansed".

Just as the lover's view of the world is coloured by the underlying force which is driving him or her, the person who has had a mystical experience will probably think that a religious view of the world is the best way of experiencing reality. So it was for me. I started out thinking that scientific questions were the most important and came to realise that religious questions were more important.

So much for questions—what about answers? Having such an experience does not furnish the answer to prob-lems or provide a reservoir of grace to make you good. But it does remind you constantly how distorted is our normal way of looking at our experience.

Remembering that the 'ground of our being' or the 'image of God' within us is there, helps us to confess our inadequacy. That is the first and necessary condition for worship.

There are many ways of worshipping, from tilling the soil which is teeming with life and tiny creatures, to turning telescopes into the far reaches of the cosmos. To the outsider who does not share the mode of experience, the activity of a worshipper is meaningless. Heads bowed in prayer are snoozing people; the soaring melody of the violin concerto is the scraping of cat gut on horse hair. We each make our choice according to our interests.

My interests were showbiz, the media and the church and so I joined the Black and White Minister show, the longest running heavy entertainment show on earth. I became ordained as a minister, worked in religious broadcasting and occasionally strayed into the green grass pastures of current affairs and the supernatural. Now I enjoy the open range of the printed page and the broadcast airwave.

I don't honestly believe that any one of these areas is more religious than another. The Church starts with an advantage because there is no substitute for meeting people who start from the advantage of realising their handicap, but sometimes they fall victim to self-righteousness or to the image projected on to them from outsiders—"they *ought* to be better".

(What they mean is that they are happy to judge others by higher standards but would not want to be subject to scrutiny themselves.) The Church also provides 'means of grace' by which God may be experienced.

Yet the voice of God is seldom heard clearly by any of us. It is coloured by a human voice. Even the still small voice of conscience by which God can also speak to us is coloured by upbringing. Culture brings other background shades into the picture. The filtering lens of human personality in all its different forms and the system of ideas which we have inherited—these are all modifying the mystic window on the world.

Far from seeing the face behind the window, we see a reflection of our own. Yet because of what I saw on a sunny afternoon in St Andrews, I believe that there is someone out there, listening in the darkness. □